AETHERNA IPSE SVAE MENTIS SIMVLACHRA LVTHERVS
EXPRIMIT AT VVLTVS CERA LVCAE OCCIDVOS
·M·D·X·X·

MARTIN LUTHER AS A MONK

THE LEGACY OF LUTHER

Martin Luther and the Reformation in the estimation of the German Lutherans from Luther's death to the beginning of the age of Goethe

by

ERNST WALTER ZEEDEN

Lecturer in Modern History in the University of Freiburg im Breisgau, Germany

LONDON
HOLLIS & CARTER

THIS translation from the original German, *Martin Luther und die Reformation im Urteil des deutschen Luthertums*—I. Band: *Darstellung* (Verlag Herder, Freiburg im Breisgau, 1950), was made by

RUTH MARY BETHELL

Made and printed in Great Britain at The Chapel River Press, Andover, Hants for Hollis & Carter Ltd., 25, Ashley Place, S.W.1

First published 1954

PREFACE TO THE ENGLISH EDITION

MY surprise was not inconsiderable when some time ago I received word that a British publishing house was planning to bring out a translation of my book on the German Lutherans. I reflected whether it was not too much to ask of a British public that it should concern itself with a specifically German aspect of the Reformation problems; for a German student they are burning enough, the whole course of Lutheran Protestantism being so closely interwoven with the history of his fatherland—but naturally of less actuality to members of other nations.

It is true, matters of more general interest are also treated, and not only those concerning internal German history, but others that have universal application, and these are, I suppose, not only the more interesting in themselves, but they provide points of contact with the Reformation in other lands in the sixteenth and seventeenth centuries. For all the reforming movements of that period had one thing in common: that they put the question of the true Church and the true Faith in a new form and gave their own decisive answers. If I am right, this is a question that still to-day occupies the thoughts of divided Christendom. Or there would be no sense in holding in Lund an Œcumenical World Conference to debate in all earnestness and solemnity the problem of Faith and Order.

The Œcumenical idea is a provoking one, and Christendom is more alive to it now than ever before. The prominent part taken by the various Churches and denominations of English-speaking countries in the world-conferences of our century is too well known to require special mention here. But the official pronouncements of the Holy See, the Pastoral Letters of not a few Catholic bishops, the sympathy and active participation of many individual Catholics, all point to the fact that the unity-seeking movements in World Protestantism are followed by the Church of Rome with keenest interest, far more so than had hitherto been known. To-day's Œcumenical misgivings and aspirations derive from an awareness that all Christian communions and confessions are of the deepest concern to one another, and that it is culpable negligence for one to be indifferent to the fate of another.

Seen in this perspective, the history and individuality of all confessions is for all confessions a matter of profound interest—an interest far removed from curiosity. It was precisely interest of that kind which provoked the writing of this book—as a modest attempt to gain from a study of Protestant sources insight into certain of the principles on which Evangelical life and thought were grounded within Lutheranism.

In order to enable all who wish to do so to check my interpretation of events and documents, in the German edition a second volume has been prepared reproducing the texts of the more important documents on which the work is based. When the original text was in Latin, this is reproduced with a parallel German translation. For the English edition this second volume has not been translated, and scholars and students of the period are referred to the German edition.[1]

In comparison, the English text is somewhat more concise. It is a pleasure to me to inform my English readers that it is to a fellow-countrywoman of theirs that is due not only the translation but in the main the present form of the book. Mrs. Ruth Mary Bethell, whose activities on the continental mainland since the end of the war have given her an excellent acquaintance with conditions of life in Austria and Germany, has in agreement with publishers and author, with rare insight and understanding, abridged certain parts of the book. It has grown somewhat slimmer, but has suffered no change of structure.

Thus, in greeting my English readers, I should like at the same time to thank the translator, with whom the author has found it both delightful and instructive to work.

ERNST WALTER ZEEDEN

Freiburg, August 16th, 1952

[1] E. W. Zeeden: *Martin Luther und die Reformation im Urteil des deutschen Luthertums*, II. Band, *Dokumente zur inneren Entwicklung des deutschen Protestantismus*, 1952. Verlag Herder, Freiburg i. Br., Germany.

CONTENTS

PART III

THE EIGHTEENTH CENTURY: THE AGE OF THE *AUFKLÄRUNG*

ILLUSTRATIONS

FOREWORD

The secret of a nation's history is revealed in its religion. ·
EICHENDORFF.

THE subject of this book is Luther and the Reformation in the estimation of Lutheran Germany, from Luther's death to the end of the eighteenth century.

It is confined to the opinions of Lutherans. Opinions of Calvinists, Catholics, or others, are omitted, as the purpose is simply to discover how the Lutherans and the Lutheran Church pictured their Luther.

What is Lutheran Protestantism, and how does it account for itself? That is the question. The last word falls to Martin Luther himself, just as in Catholic matters the last word falls to the Catholics and Catholicism.

It was after the long and lonely struggle during which he worked out his interpretation of the Gospel that Luther grew conscious of being a messenger of God. In a world in turmoil, but still wholly Christian, he identified *his* doctrine with Christianity, *his* cause with God's, and held to his identification passionately, naïvely; and this is how the Reformation and the Evangelical Church began.

As far as Protestant Germany is concerned, the way a man comes to terms with his Luther is a sure indication of what sort of Christian he is. This is what makes the reformer different from other men of genius in Germany; for no other dared to claim that his work was God's work, and that the eternal salvation or damnation of men depended on their believing in it; not Frederick the Great, not Beethoven, not Goethe, not Leibniz.

In Germany, the changing picture of Luther through the decades and centuries has one constant factor, in that it is a reflex of religious ideas. The changes are indications of spiritual evolutions, and if it is indeed true that a nation's religious movements tell its innermost history, then light on the successive transformations undergone by Luther and the Reformation, in the minds of successive generations, is bound to show some portion of the road along which the German nation—or a part of it—travelled.

The sixteenth-, seventeenth- and eighteenth-century texts on which this study is based form a selection only of the complete Lutheran literature of the period covered (1546–1800). It was not the author's intention to exhaust the subject, but merely to record the change of perspective at each stage. The relevant texts are listed in a special index and transcribed at length in a second volume, where they are available for special studies. (This volume has not been translated into English.)

Up to a century and a half after his death, literature on Luther is almost wholly the work of theologians. Towards the end of the seventeenth century, thoughtful laymen first embarked on theological studies, and Seckendorf wrote his *History of Lutheranism*. But from 1550 to 1700 Luther is the subject of dogmatic theology and confessional controversy; the theme is his doctrine rather than his person.

Orthodoxy from its inception in the sixteenth century to its full development in the seventeenth saw the Reformation to all intents and purposes from one standpoint only, that of revelation. This accounts for much repetition among the authors of the period, but no one minded this at the time, and the unanimity of thought only served to stress the common source behind it all. So we cover the second and above all the third chapter of Part I. The latter, on the seventeenth century, brings out most clearly how a completely uniform conception of Luther and the Reformation existed in the minds of all, princes, preachers, strict theologians and popular writers on theological matters.

In 1700 or a little earlier, pietistic ideas began to predominate, and the reformer became a bone of contention in Evangelical inter-confessional disputations. It was at this time that philosophy became aware of him. Laymen not only expressed opinions, often a purely secular attitude was adopted. In the trials of strength between Christians and philosophers, which were to intensify and spread in the eighteenth century, Luther stands in a remarkable double light, for to one side he was the man of progress, to the other the man of faith, both sides claiming allegiance to the one Luther. The stream of his followers became more various: alongside the strict dogmatic theologians of the seventeenth-century type, we have the more conciliatory schools of pietistic and ' enlightened ' theology, some critical, some loyal. And along with the theologians we have the non-theologians, intellectuals and professionals of all sorts. Luther is now the subject-matter of Evangelical apologetics, of progressive philosophy, of pragmatic historical studies; he engages the attention of humanistic as well as religious thought. Pietism brought about an intensification of individual religious life, and the emphasis was on Luther's personal characteristics. The tendency was to see in him the archetype of the religious aspirations dominant at the time.

The German classical period tended to overlook the obvious connection between the reformer and the founding of the reformed Church. Herder was among the first who took to describing Luther in terms of genius, mentioning him in the same breath as Shakespeare and Michelangelo. Goethe said the Reformation was of no importance, the only fact of interest being the character of Luther; and Fichte says (in his ' Eighth Address to the German Nation '): ' Noteworthy about the first Protestants was not the content of their belief but the determination with which they stood up for it.'

The natural link between the German Protestant and Luther's doctrine and reformation was overlooked in the eighteenth century and by the nineteenth was no longer taken for granted. Detach Luther from his doctrine, and it is easy to turn him into a forerunner of intellectual freedom or nationalistic ideas.

To sum up, in the sixteenth and seventeenth centuries it was the theologians who studied Luther; in the eighteenth century the philosophizing members of the schools, chief among them the historians. So the one-time rouser of violent passions became the object of supposedly impartial scientific investigations. . . .

PART I

THE AGE OF RELIGIOUS
CONTROVERSY AND ORTHODOXY

INTRODUCTION

LUTHER'S ACCOUNT OF HIMSELF

LUTHER's evidence on himself is to be found in innumerable scattered references in his works. Each resounds with that personal note which no one who heard it ever forgot. In Germany, to know these passages is part of a liberal education. For all their depth and abundance, the underlying principle is never lost sight of. Luther had the knack of plunging without preamble to the heart and rock-bottom of his subject. The best example is his Table-talk.

His reader is brought so swiftly, so surely into touch with the very essence of his faith, his life, his thought, that he soon becomes aware of what a deep, richly-endowed spirit it is that controls such abundant output. Whatever texts are chosen, Luther's account of himself remains constant, the individual note is struck forcibly all the time.

As it seemed to him, the revealing of his gospel had thrown such a flood of light on the contemporary scene that earlier times sank into deep shadow.

> Our gospel has, praise God, done a lot of good [he wrote in 1531 to 'his dear Germans']; till now, no one has known what the Gospel is, or what Christ, baptism, . . . God, Church, a Christian . . . are. In fact we did not know what a Christian ought to know. The papal asses darkened and suppressed it all. Asses they are indeed . . . , for I was one too . . .

However that may be, what was accomplished in little over a decade of preaching remains, he claims, astounding: people of every age and sex learnt their catechism afresh and knew what living and dying in the faith meant; and the visible Church was again apparent. Still more astonishing is what Luther expected of the near future. In a letter sent from the fortress of Coburg to Augsburg, to his friends Melanchthon, Spalatin, Jonas and

Agricola, he predicted that the *Confessio Augustana* would force a way into the courts of all princes and monarchs, would rule in the midst of its enemies and spread throughout the whole world, so there would be no more excuse for any who remained unbelievers.

Luther himself, and under his stimulus the whole body of preachers caught up by the Reformation, introduced a new style of preaching the Gospel. It was meant at the time to be a revival of the original Christian message. It differed from mediæval preaching chiefly in one respect, in that it declared the doctrine of the Universal Church to be the mere work of man (and therefore not binding) and drew its subject matter from the Bible direct, independently of doctrine. This was made possible by the new attitude to the Middle Ages: the authority of the Church had been superseded by the authority of conscience.

Conscience, as Luther meant it, differs on several points from the conception of conscience with which we are familiar since the eighteenth century. ' To act against conscience is not allowed,' Luther pronounced in 1521 at the Diet of Worms. In the same statement he declared that conscience is bound up in God's word. ' Neither bishop nor pope, nor any man whatever, has the right to prescribe a single syllable to any Christian, even with his own consent.' Conscience was only freed by Christ (or by Scripture) from obedience to pope or doctrine in order that Christ should reign supreme over it. It is that part of a man where God makes man aware of him, so that to act against conscience is to act against God.

This conscience it was that drove Luther to prefer his own reading of Scripture to that of the Church, and to proclaim it as the pure clear gospel: a guiding principle of the Reformation and of its subsequent development. It led to the forced abdication of the Church in favour of the Bible. Early as well as later Christianity had taken the holy scriptures of the Old and New Testament as the source of faith. But that was no guarantee that individual and even fundamental passages were not open to various explanations. When the theologians came across inter-pretations that touched on principles of faith (as for instance in the cases of Arius and his theory on the sonship of Christ) the Church was accustomed to take action through council and pope, and to declare specifically what was in conformity with doctrine and what was not.

Luther was not breaking new ground when he turned to the Bible, but only when he cut the Bible off from Pope and Church, or subordinated them. In questions of faith, he said, what was decisive was neither Pope nor council but the witness of the Scriptures alone. He even went so far as to maintain that Satan himself inspired the doctrine by which a man may not read his own meaning into the Scriptures, for in Scripture alone was to be found the spirit by which Scripture was to be understood. ' I have no wish to be known as a man more learned than others,' he stated in 1521, ' but I wish Scripture to be sovereign, and not interpreted according to my mind or the mind of another, but interpreted by itself in its own spirit.' So he did not consider what he taught to be the product of his own mind, but of Scripture, that is, God. Thus alone can we explain the sweeping identification of God's word and Luther's doctrine so prevalent in his works. In the letters from Coburg to Augsburg (1530) he never tired of persuading his friends that the *Confessio Augustana* was dealing not with Luther's cause but God's. ' *Causa nostra est justa et vera denique ipsius Christi et Dei,*' are his very words in one of the innumerable letters to Melanchthon. To Chancellor Brück he wrote on August 5, 1530:

> God cannot forget us, he must needs first forget himself. For that would mean our cause were not his cause and our word not his word. But we are convinced and are without doubt that it is his cause and his word, and thus our prayer is surely heard and help is at hand.

His opponents he saw as presumptuous men who dared to defy God; he called them enemies of God and the Gospel and held fast to his crystal-clear and stark conviction till his dying day. The same formula reappears in his last major work: *Against the Papacy founded by the Devil* (1545): ' He who is against our evangelion is against the cause of God and His Spirit.'

If the ' pure clear gospel ' of Martin Luther differed from the Roman Church on several points of doctrine, other points were common to both. Luther's doctrine of the non-freedom of the human will in matters concerning the salvation of the soul, and that on the twofold species of the Sacrament of the Lord's Supper were fundamental to him; but still more important was the doctrine he deduced from St. Paul, of the sinner's justification by faith: this belief it was that brought him relief at last in his agonizingly bitter struggle as a monk.

Note that when he says gospel, he means justification by faith. He traced Christianity back to this concept, he identified Christianity and the true Church with it. ' Head and corner-stone,' he called his justification articles, it alone ' begot the Church, nourished it, raised it up, protected and defended it,' and furthermore, without it, God's Church could not exist a single hour. Indeed the Church Fathers who were ignorant of it never attained to knowledge of the truth. The importance he attached to his idea cannot be too strongly emphasized. ' Take away the justification article,' he wrote in 1531, ' and you do away with the Church, for it can then withstand no error. Except within this article the Holy Ghost neither will nor can be with us.' Hence he thought it better for the world to perish than that it should be questioned. ' Should the world go stark mad, still it would have to leave the article standing, though it fall itself down to the bottom of Hell. Amen.' ' As concerns this article, one cannot slacken or yield, though heaven or earth fall, or fall what may.' ' The justification article is the lord and prince of all forms of doctrine and rules all conscience and the whole Church. Without it the world is stale and naught but darkness; no error but will steal in and rule, be it absent.'

So the Gospel itself was reduced to this one doctrine, and Luther was possessed of the assurance it was God's word and deeply convinced that not to accept it was to blaspheme against God.

He sought for it in vain in Church dogma and in the writings of the Fathers, and not finding it there he convinced himself that the papacy, the representative embodiment of the Church, was the seat of Antichrist. ' For what is not of God must be of the

Devil.' His fight against the papacy grew ever more intense and fierce because he fancied he found Satan in it. The historic strife of Christ with the Devil and Antichrist, as in *Thessalonians* ii, 2, and in the *Apocalypse*, he saw in actual process in his own controversies with the pope. To his mind, his friends in Augsburg were fighting, not against men, but against the gates of Hell. The confusion prophesied in *Matthew* xxiv, where it is written: ' Many false prophets and christs will arise and say: Here is Christ, and will lead many astray; do not believe them,' he identified in all seriousness with the wrongful leadership ' which now governs under the name of the Roman Church,' and he considered himself divinely called to tell his contemporaries and later generations how he had unmasked the accursed Antichrist in the person of the pope.

Luther saw himself always as the instrument of God appointed for a special function in the process of salvation. It was a process that began with Adam, reached the fullness of time with the Incarnation, and entered its final course at the Ascension, continuing—and still continuing to-day for the believer—to culminate in the Second Coming of Christ and the Last Judgement. Satan will be judged and condemned on the last day. Till then he will be given free play in the world. He uses the opportunity to interfere with the work of redemption begun by God through Christ and to be completed in the final stage of the history of the redemption. This was the background against which Luther saw himself and his work, and against which his disciples saw him—and his opponents too, the papists, with the sole difference that they scented out Satan the seducer in Luther himself and defended the Roman Church as the tabernacle of God on earth.

Later times were to honour in him the man of genius, the national hero, the pioneer of progress. For him, his mission was a religious one and nothing else. So much so that the many scandalous rumours touching his person did not disturb him at all, he said. ' But let no one ask patience and favour of me who would make of my Lord Christ preached by me, and of the Holy Ghost, agents of falsehood. It is of no consequence, but I will be answerable for God's word with a joyous heart and good cheer.'

To sum up, his mission was to preach the Gospel, but his gospel was confined to the doctrine of justification by faith alone. Such was his reading of Holy Scripture. His conscience was assured that this was Christ's teaching. His conscience drove him to obey Scripture as understood by him rather than Scripture as understood by the Roman Church, and indeed to break with the Roman Church. The break was the beginning of the Reformation.

The break with the Catholic—universal—Roman Church was not caused solely by differences of opinion on the justification dogma. It began at an even deeper level. A comparison between the two following questions makes this clear: what was it that induced Luther to take up his particular form of belief (that is, the justification article and all that goes with it)? And, what is the origin of the creed of the Roman Church (its dogma)? Luther traced his back to his experience, and his conscience vouched for its authenticity. The Roman Church found and finds its creed, together with all statements on matters of faith, grounded in the New Testament and inspired by the Holy Spirit himself; for according to St. John the disciples were promised they would receive the Holy Spirit, and according to the *Acts of the Apostles* the Spirit descended on them at the first Pentecost. And St. John it is who states that when the Lord has left them, the Spirit, the Comforter, will guide them into all truth, being himself the spirit of truth.

So we might have been spared the painful dilemma which still divides present-day Christendom. But because Luther, as a single individual, upheld a different faith from that of the entire mystical body of Christ, and because he as a single individual heeded only his conscience and not the Church as a whole, and because, moreover, at the time a large part of Christendom was on his side, the Church, united till then, broke asunder.

The cause of the break, though one in Luther's mind, was in fact twofold: first a new guiding principle, which we may call freedom of conscience, set up in the place of the theocentric principle of the Holy Spirit; secondly a new form of belief: the doctrine of justification by faith alone, in lieu of the old doctrine (newly formulated at the Tridentine Council) of justification by faith and good will. However, conscience and doctrine are two quite different things with no inevitable connections. Later, Lutheran orthodoxy was to hold only the doctrine to be authoritative; pietism and rationalism, on the other hand, only the primacy of personal religious experience and freedom from manmade codes.

How far both ideas, reciprocally or alternately, contributed to a standard picture of the reformer and determined the creed of his Church, will, we hope, become evident in the course of this work.

CHAPTER I
LUTHER'S FRIENDS AND ASSOCIATES

1. JOHANNES BUGENHAGEN, JUSTUS JONAS, MICHAEL COELIUS, HANS SACHS

THOSE of Luther's contemporaries who knew him well and were nearest to him left a number of personal impressions, but not a single clear picture of him. All these documents, however personal in tone, point away from his person to stress his mission.

Whereas we other preachers creep and stammer beside him, he sets forth boldly as upon an open sea and has at his command an ocean of words and deeds whence we draw mere droplets. . . . He can make all things straight where we all together can do nothing.[1]

Bugenhagen is a grammarian and spreads the power of the word, whereas I, Melanchthon, am a logician and show up relationships and provide proofs, Justus Jonas is a rhetorician, finely and richly endowed; but Luther is all in all, a miracle among men; what he says and writes grips the heart and leaves a marvellous deep impression behind.

His death was the occasion for his friends to speak out exhaustively in sermons and funeral orations. The year 1546 saw the first small biographies—all with a breath of personal warmth. The lament is no sooner voiced than it is drowned in candid consolation. And so it was with his personality: he was mentioned but to vanish again, the effect he produced was superhuman. Hans Sachs made an effort to stress the human and personal characteristics, calling him loyal, constant, true, bold and fearless, chivalrous, a warrior of God hazarding his life. So was he in the eyes of his followers. And to some extent in actual fact. Justus Jonas, the professor, was concerned with intellectual rather than popular traits:

[1] Jonas.

He was of keen intelligence and remarkably high powers of reason . . . and had also . . . many other abundant gifts and was an excellent powerful speaker, to wit a superlative powerful interpreter of the word. . . . The pulpits too have some of them learnt from him how to speak and write the German tongue aright.

The deep and quite unique impression which his personality left on his contemporaries is undeniable; but the secret of his power lies elsewhere, as Bugenhagen discloses: '. . . the man is indeed departed in Christ but the powerful holy godly doctrine of this beloved man now lives more than ever strong.' And again: ' Through him has Christ now conquered for nearly thirty years.'

This, taken at its face value, implies that Luther's doctrine, reformation and all, was not his human achievement but was brought about by God: an act of God, an act of grace, upon Church and world, using Luther as a tool. Just as God spoke, taught through Luther, so in the last resort it is God who is honoured in Luther. He was called preacher of the truth[1] and apostolic warrior[2]—but that is nothing; Coelius is at pains to show that Luther had a mission that differed not at all from the mission of Elias, Jeremias and John the Baptist. Bugenhagen goes one better and describes Luther as an angel. Not just any angel, but the one of which it is written in the fourteenth chapter of the *Apocalypse*, that John saw him flying in mid-heaven, bearing an eternal gospel to proclaim to all men, peoples and nations. ' That angel that cried: Fear God and give him the praise! was D. Martin Luther.'

All this is proof of the immense gravity with which his gospel was received. Apostles, prophets and angels are, in their mediæval sense, and in fact in every Christian sense, ambassadors with a special mission to fulfil within God's mandate for mankind.

Luther's mission, as his contemporaries saw it, was simply, and in deadly earnest, the re-establishment of the Gospel ' all clear and pure as in the beginning,' doctrine purified, the preaching of honest repentance, confession and forgiveness of sins, as

---

[1] Jonas. [2] Hans Sachs.

it was and shall be.[1] But the negative side to his mission cannot be ignored: the call to destroy all enemies of the pure doctrine through God's word. Christ's eternal foe, Satan, was detected raging, roaring and seducing in the ranks of the papacy, intent on hurling the souls of Christians down into hell. This is an absolutely vital point: Rome as the diabolical mint of false currency was Luther's great discovery and the cause of his attacks on papacy and Church. Significantly, Bugenhagen, at the end of his Luther oration, called for prayer that God would make Luther's prophecy come true—the one he himself composed as an inscription for his own tombstone: ' *Pestis eram vivus, moriens tua mors ero, Papa!* ' ' O Pope, living I was your plague, dying I shall be your bitter death. May God be praised for ever and ever through Jesus Christ our Lord. Amen.'

Luther was compared to the prophets as a matter of course, and to the men of God of the Old Testament and Church history; it was taken as equally obvious that the pope was to be equated with the servants of Baal, the worshippers of idols and the foes of God.

In his day Elias assaulted and overthrew idolatry, and Martin Luther fell upon the powerful idol of papal indulgence and hurled it to the ground. Elias killed the priests of Baal, and Luther the man of God overthrew the Mass-priests and their idol with the sword of the divine word.[1]

So great was the gulf between Luther and his associates, and Church doctrine. His attitude to the Roman Church had an important influence on the development of his own church. The views of his contemporaries are stark and plain. Hans Sachs sees Holy Theology in snowy garments approaching Luther's bier and voicing her apprehensions: she fears she will be dragged in the mire again now he is gone.

It was not long before Evangelical church history was teaching that through Martin Luther the Roman pope had been unmasked as the real Antichrist, and taught it with all the zeal of conviction at Protestant universities for over two hundred years.

[1] Coelius.

Contemporary preaching on Antichrist was impulsive rather than dogmatic. Antichrist, the devil, the Roman Church, the sects of enthusiasts and Baptists were all tarred with the same brush as foes of pure godly doctrine. God working through Luther and Satan through the Roman pope. The last important work of the reformer points to the devil as the founder of the papacy. All evil in the world can be traced to Satan, and everything satanic was somehow related to the papacy and hence to the Roman Church.

It went amiss with the Church under the papal Antichrist [says Coelius]. There was no proper understanding of Holy Writ, no right doctrine was preached for the solace of conscience; man-made codes were esteemed above the word of God, no one knew how to invoke God, or how to turn to him in trouble, what to do or how to serve him. Darkness covered the whole face of the earth, no light shone in the Church.

Laxity of morals and neglect of Church doctrine had been condemned and attempts made to combat them a hundred years before Luther. So this is not a sixteenth-century innovation but good late mediæval tradition. The same applies to the interpretation of contemporary events in terms of apocalyptic ideas. What was new, and at the same time a token of the reformed church's sense of mission, is that it saw the biblical Antichrist prophecies fulfilled in the papacy and had no qualms in drawing its conclusions.

These ideas dominated the interpretation of history in Evangelical circles. In Christian thought history is the history of salvation, God working in time among men, with its end and completion in the Last Judgement. Whatever happens on earth is part of the history of salvation. And though diabolical and heavenly powers play their part, as the *Apocalypse* shows, man is the immediate and visible agent. In the sixteenth century this was the commonly accepted view. Reformed Christianity, however, brought it into sharp outline, with Luther and the pope as apocalyptic figures, and salvation a very present issue of their duel, witnessed against a background of eternity; wrestling powers of heaven and hell were almost within reach—the outcome was to decide for God or devil.

John and the prophets were writing about Luther and the pope. The pope as Antichrist, Luther as Elias or John the Baptist, who were to appear again, risen from the dead, before the end of the world; or he was one of the apocalyptic angels. But all these appear only when the end is near; so it was concluded that the Day of Judgement was at hand. The phrase ' in these latter times' constantly recurs. Belief in Antichrist, so strong in the mediæval Church, was thus given an out-and-out Protestant imprint.

2. MELANCHTHON

Of all Luther's contemporaries, Melanchthon gives us the clearest and most rounded picture of him. He gave the funeral oration for the university of Wittenberg and composed a biography as introduction to the second volume of the Wittenberg edition of Luther's works (June 1546). He has the same standpoint as his contemporaries, but he is a man with a fine, cultivated, shrewd, humanistic mind who excelled in learning and breadth of vision. His relation to reformation and reformer was less simple and guileless, but thoughtful and balanced.

He stood very near to Luther but their friendship was not without clouds owing to the difference in character and temperament. Luther often attacked Melanchthon ruthlessly. The latter seldom retaliated. All the bitterness the shrewd, sensitive don had stored up in him came to light only after Luther's death. He dared to take exception to certain aspects of the reformer's doctrine and person. In April 1548 he wrote in no uncertain terms to the Saxon Councillor Christoph v. Carlowitz, who enquired about his attitude to Church union as proposed at the so-called *Augsburg Interim*; he said the Elector should do as he saw fit; he, Melanchthon, would submit.

After all in Luther's time I was often compelled to give in and found it more than humiliating. He would drive away at his point, out of sheer passionate obstinacy, with little regard for what befitted his person or the common weal.

The cry of one driven to the wall. Melanchthon, however, never forgot that the man whose stronger will had beaten him down was a very remarkable man with exceptional powers. Elsewhere he broke a lance for his rough aggressive manner: it was God's intention to strike fear into the insolent foe and to provide a harsh and thorough surgeon for 'the crimes of these latter days.' He greatly esteemed Luther and dwelt on his conformity of preaching and practice, of word and deed.

His virtue and wisdom he rated so highly that he considered human powers alone could never have attained to such heights: they were gifts of God. The same he held to be true of the main lines of his doctrine: it lay so far beyond human grasp that God himself must have taught him.

(a) MELANCHTHON'S VIEW OF LUTHER'S MISSION

Typical of his times in this respect, Melanchthon saw Luther with all his idiosyncrasies as touched with the creative power of the personal Christian God. He was 'called and chosen by God specially to help the churches to recover.' When you think of him, he told his audience at the funeral oration, you must distinguish between the virtues he possessed and the office he held in the church. The latter is the more important. In the book of *Nehemiah*[1] (iv, 11) he found the prototype he needed. Just as the Jews after the return from exile in Babylon built the temple in Jerusalem under attack from the enemy, building with one hand, with the other brandishing the sword, so had he defended the Gospel against the enemy and built up his church by preaching and expounding the Bible for the comfort of the people.

Melanchthon undertook to work out an historical law valid for world and Church, which would show up the part in history allotted to the German reformer; St. Paul in his *Epistle to the*

[1] 2 *Esdras* in the Vulgate.

Ephesians describes Christ ascended and seated on the right hand of the Father, bestowing gifts on mankind, and Melanchthon deduces the following: 'It is comfortable and profitable to observe how God had the Church in mind from the very beginning, sending sound teachers in due order, just as in the order of battle those in the front rank withdraw as soon as others have come to occupy their positions and follow in their traces.' The first fathers came in turn: Adam, Seth, Enoch, Methusalem, and so on, in an unbroken sequence down to the Macchabees, Simeon, John the Baptist, to Christ himself and the apostles. 'It is profitable to consider this order and sequence; for it is a clear indication of the presence of God in the Church.' Since the apostles, Catholics hold that God works in the world through the Church, the mystical body of Christ with its members, right down to the present time. It is unlikely that Melanchthon had any doubt about this. But he stressed the importance of the renewal and revival of the Church through men of God and God's action through men with an historic mission.

After the apostles came the crowd of Church Fathers and teachers, who although not actually ranking as apostles and prophets still bore marks of holiness, such as Polycarp, Irenaeus, Gregory, Thaumaturgos, Basil, Augustine, Prosper, Maxim, Hugo Bernard, Tauler, with many others in other places. And although these latter days are more wicked, nonetheless God has never left men in the lurch and the light of the Gospel shines out brighter and purer than ever through Luther's words. He should therefore be counted among the number and order of the exalted men whom God sent to earth to gather his Church together and restore it. We must understand that such people are to be considered as the finest flower of the human race on earth . . .

Fundamental to Melanchthon's idea of Luther is this law of history by which God manifests his presence to certain chosen people, formerly the Jews, since Christ the Christians, through special charisma-bearers; the belief that Luther was such an one is implicit in his reduction of Church history to a mere history of 'God's messengers.' But Melanchthon was a man of the Middle Ages in so far as he saw events symbolically: he looked for the meaning behind the facts.

(b) MELANCHTHON'S ATTITUDE TO THE ROMAN CHURCH AND THE REFORMATION

Melanchthon does not come out so strongly as an opponent of the papacy as his more bellicose Evangelical brethren. An opinion on the reformer necessarily involved one of the Roman Church, and in the sixteenth century a positive attitude to the former meant a negative one to the latter. Critical remarks about the old Church abound. Melanchthon accused it of practices which he said Luther had eliminated: ceremonies and an Aristotelian philosophy. Ritual appeared to him a series of childish acts hindering the proper approach to God; the original Church doctrine had been altered, Aristotelianism was a poisonous accretion which distorted the Gospel.

Since Albert, Thomas Aquinas, and Duns Scotus, the Church was sodden with errors. Luther combated them and declared himself free, but the official Church held fast and this is the cause of the break. He deemed it painful and unchristian. The fault, however, lay not with Luther but with the Roman Church. ' If such unhappiness comes from disunity—as we see indeed with great sorrow that much unhappiness has come—the fault lies with those who sowed errors in the first place, and who now defend them with diabolical hatred.'

It was because he enacted the Reformation and had, in Evangelical terms, brought the Church back to its original true state, that Luther was accorded superhuman honours. Contemporaries and later devotees held that the Gospel had not been preached in so clear and pure a form since the time of the apostles.[1] Melanchthon was more cautious and took pains to provide reasons for his allegiance.

There was the incontestable success of Luther's preaching: ' Luther it was who recalled the hearts of men to the Son of

[1] Coelius.

God '; with Luther's interpretation of the Bible ' in the judgement of all pious and judicious people,' a light had arisen after a long dark night. Luther was a light because he had delved so deeply into the meaning of the Gospel and distinguished between law and evangelium, and unlike the official Church he 'lay hold upon the whole doctrine necessary to salvation and restored purity of morals.'

The Evangelical faith was none other than the real eternal doctrine of the *Catholica Ecclesia Dei*, ' in accordance with which the prayer and life of a Christian must be conducted.' It was the same doctrine of which the Son of God speaks: ' He who loves me keeps my word and my Father will love him and we will come to him and take our abode with him.'[1] It was therefore right to keep it alive in men's minds and to let it be known.

Thanks were due to God for Luther's mission, for ' through him the light of the Gospel has been lit for us anew.'

3. JOHANNES MATHESIUS

The human touches, personal reminiscences and occasional anecdotes in contemporary accounts of Luther's life and work give them life and authenticity. The authors loved Luther, the man foretold in the apocalyptical passages of the Bible as specially chosen by God to reveal Antichrist was the friend with whom they worked and sat at table, and who sometimes in the evening played the lute. This nearness, which the most awe-inspired sense of distance could not efface—or rather both the sense of proximity and that of remoteness—contributed much to the picture of Luther which they handed down: historically great and humanly touching, something of the spell remains in the biographical writings, a last breath of it in the sermons on his life which Johannes Mathesius preached between 1562 and 1565 in Joachimsthal. These, seventeen in number, were published in Nuremberg in 1566. It is the last work from Luther's immediate circle and the first great biography.

Mathesius was born in 1504, a few years later than

[1] *John* xiv, 23.

Melanchthon. He was a student in Wittenberg during the decisive years of the Reformation, between 1520 and 1530, so he knew the Luther of the fighting days and declared he had at times shared his table. He took his Master's degree and was appointed to the parish of Joachimsthal in Bohemia, where a bare twenty years after the reformer's death he preached a series of sermons and had them printed in German, ' to the honour of God and blessed German theology.' At the age of sixty he confessed himself happy to have been a disciple of Luther and Melanchthon in the ' high school of learning ' in Wittenberg. He sings the praises of Wittenberg so loud that one concludes his experience there was profound and decisive.

' Many people alive to-day have no idea how it was fifty years ago in the oppressed and fettered Church, and certain thankless folk are ready utterly to forget this great man and his steady hard work and achievement.' To honour and praise God and render thanks to him, and to bear witness to true Christian religion: this was the best way of paying tribute to Luther's memory; moreover comfort was in it and admonition to right doctrine for contemporaries and younger men. Purely human admiration for the reformer himself lends freshness and colour to the whole biography.

Mathesius did not make lists of Luther's qualities as orthodox theologians were to do, he let them appear out of a given situation. He liked to dwell affectionately on this or that characteristic or occurrence as suitable for imitation and edification. He was not alone in stressing Martin Luther's Christian example, as for instance in the conformity between what he said and what he did. ' Although life and good example cannot make the doctrine any better, it is seemly and conducive to the furtherance of doctrine if the preacher lead a sober Christian life.' He did not argue about Luther's attacks of misgiving as orthodox writers and the *Aufklärung* were to do, but described an encounter between Luther and a woman:

' Do you remember the creed you learnt as a child? ' he asked. ' Yes,' said the woman, and repeated it with admirable piety. 'Do you still believe it is true?' asked Luther. And when she answered, 'Yes,' he said: 'Truly, dear woman, if you hold and believe this word to be true, so that it is nothing but true, then your faith is stronger than mine. For I must every day pray for an increase in my faith.' Whereupon the woman thanked God and went away full of peace and joy.

In the words of Duke George of Saxony, he praised the frankness of ' those of Wittenberg,' ' who are not mealy-mouthed but speak out their minds truly and fully.' There was still no set profile of the reformer for general recognition, and Mathesius knew well enough that the man who posted his theses in Wittenberg enjoyed a drink with friends and after the Bible was fond of Æsop's fables and of children and animals.

Luther's main achievement, as Mathesius saw, was his ' doctrine,' but his own bent was to the cure of souls rather than to teaching, and he valued Luther's practical directives more highly than his learned theological writings. If in all his life Luther had done nothing worth while beyond introducing the two catechisms and the habit of saying grace before and after food, ' and on going to bed and getting up . . . the whole world could never thank him and repay him sufficiently.'

Like Melanchthon, he particularly valued Luther's teaching on civic authority. Melanchthon found it useful for admonishing men how to render to God what is God's and to Cæsar what is Cæsar's, and valued axiomatic passive obedience so highly that he wrote: ' When I consider in my heart how on this very matter so many great churchmen have acted thoughtlessly, I take it as assured that the heart of this man was guided not by human judgement but by divine inspiration . . .'

Mathesius called Melanchthon to witness that Luther never favoured rebellion or discontent. He produced examples, told how Luther had gone down on his knees to beg the warlords to desist and make peace, and said that he spoke of ' this peaceable man's ' efforts to bring about quiet and unity ' in order to warn young preachers not to concern themselves with worldly affairs or take part in riots.' Melanchthon explained how Luther taught men to give honour to God in true worship and good conscience, and in all civic duties to submit to the existing authorities as was the will of God. On the strength of this, later writers tried to turn the reformer into something he never was: a state-server at all costs.

Mathesius took over Luther's identification of Antichrist and pope exactly as it stood, only deepening the cleft between papists and Evangelicals by setting the whole controversy within the framework of the history of the redemption.

Reviewing Luther's powerful book *Against the Papacy*, he seized the occasion to make a small defence of Luther's coarseness in attack ('The Lord . . . who has roused such heated and fiery zeal in his chosen instrument . . . will surely know how to forgive his servant '). But at heart he too held that meeting the pope was meeting the devil or Antichrist: apologies for any harshness of tone were here superfluous.

DIVINE AUTHORITY

For Mathesius and Melanchthon, history was the history of God's word in the world, from Adam onwards. Christ was the centre and Luther a last high moment before Judgement Day. One point Melanchthon forgot: Satan, God's opponent, everywhere at work all through history, active already before the Incarnation, and since Christ engaged in perpetual warfare with God and the world. Satan had blocked and poisoned the holy springs of the word since the first day, but God at given times sent ' his master-plumbers who cleaned out the choked fountains and blocked pipes and produced fresh springs of water.' It was Satan who called up ' Arius and Mohammed in the East and Antichrist in the West,' who ' destroyed " the holy aqueducts of God," so that the whole of poor Christendom suffered lack of clear fresh water and . . . the master-plumber himself, the holy fountain of life,' our Lord God, cried out in anguish. At last God founded the school and church of Wittenberg, and his pure and holy word went abroad throughout the greater part of the Roman Empire. And now the devil and his Antichrist vent their wrath against school and church.

The Diet of Augsburg (1530) was a decisive moment in the long warfare which made up the history of the redemption. He turned to the Old Testament[1] and called it the day of the sounding of trumpets: Christ, Gospel and Dr. Luther stood arraigned against devil, pope and falsehood, and the right hand of the Lord gave victory for Luther's cause against the gates of hell. In full accord with this interpretation of events was the expected end of the world shortly after God's intervention through Luther. The appearance of Antichrist is, according to the New Testament, the sign of the beginning of the end. Antichrist was in full evidence in the papacy: hence the imminence of the Last Judgement.[2]

Luther's stature had become superhuman, a mighty figure in Christian mythology, more powerful even than in his lifetime. It was Luther as a German that Mathesius liked to contemplate in apotheosis—the German prophet *par excellence*, his mission covering Germany, his function that of prophet to the Germans.

Thinking along these lines, Mathesius came to consider the mediæval idea of *Imperium*. God, he wrote, before the end of the world awarded to that same laudable German land after the bestowal of empire, crown and sceptre, a German prophet, . . . and behold, Martin Luther arose and preached. By this means God made clear his intention to reveal and destroy Antichrist and to show mercy in his visitation of the land of Germany before the Last Judgement.[3]

The memory of the fourth of Daniel's kingdoms was certainly a factor here: to the mediæval mind it was the Roman-German empire which should survive to the end of the world. Justus Jonas and others had earlier written of how John Huss had foretold the coming of a German prophet. Mathesius seized upon this legend.

[1] *Lev.* xxiii, 23 sqq.; *Num.* xxix, 1 sqq.

[2] The *Spirituals* of the late Middle Ages also held that the end of the world was near at hand, as Clemens Bauer points out, because they considered themselves exposed to oppression on the part of Antichrist.

[3] Luther as prophet of the Germans is an idea that in its secularized form was taken up again by the German national school of history in the nineteenth century.

' To-day you are roasting a goose,' said Huss in 1415, the year in which the Council of Constance condemned him to be burnt at the stake, ' but in a hundred years, that is with 1516, a real swan will come and he will at last sing you another song'— which God be praised did really come about, for in 1516 Dr. Luther began to preach against indulgences.

Mathesius called Luther a blessed instrument, a chosen weapon of God, a miracle-man; elsewhere he called his doctrine as assembled in the *Augsburg Confession* a precious and splendid witness, such that none more splendid or lofty had been seen since apostolic days; the spirit of Christ had taught at Wittenberg through Luther.

All this sprang from the sincere conviction that Luther's doctrine and God's word were one: Luther himself was thoroughly persuaded of this identity and his own assurance infected his followers.

But in that case the following implications also held good: divine authority for the doctrine; anathema on any deviations, which amounted to a betrayal of the very Gospel of God itself.

Hence, for example, Zwingli's condemnation by Luther and his followers. Mathesius described in the strongest terms how numerous poor folk had been led astray by the Swiss reformer's departure from Luther's dogma. He solemnly warned his parishioners against any attempt to add this or that novelty to Lutheran doctrine, and begged them in the name of Wittenberg, Luther and Melanchthon, to hold the Wittenberg doctrine in high honour and not to let themselves be led astray ' by every passing wind ' from the doctrine of our Lord Christ.

This emphasis on the scrupulous observance of Luther's doctrine at its most literal started the process by which Luther became uncompromisingly committed to his own statements. Later generations gathered them into a dogmatic system. Mathesius was too early for this, but the solemn words at the close of his book reveal a tendency already active, though of decisive importance mainly in the second generation of the Reformation period. It introduced a new phase of evangelical Christianity: Lutheran Orthodoxy.

CHAPTER II

THE SECOND GENERATION OF THE REFORMATION PERIOD—THE EMERGENCE OF LUTHERAN ORTHODOXY

1. MATTHIAS FLACIUS ILLYRICUS

THE second generation of the Reformation period lacked the friendly personal relationship to Martin Luther. He was a great man and his work was accomplished, and the work hid the man. There were no more disciples, the new men had not shared the hard days of Wittenberg, Worms, Speyer and Augsburg and the fights and victories between 1517 and 1530: these were historical facts, not personal experience.

The eldest of them was Matthias Flacius of Illyria (1520–75). In the fifties of the sixteenth century he was responsible for drafting the first Protestant Church history and undertook an important share of the work himself. It is called after its place of origin, the *Magdeburg Centurien*, and was the standard Lutheran history, an epoch-making publication. True, Flacius never reached the Reformation, and we have no rounded picture of Luther, but there are many useful indications of his attitude to Luther, both here and in his polemical theological writings.

His description of the expansion of the Church is gloomy in the extreme, wholly dominated by Satan of whose existence he had no shadow of doubt. The downward trend of the Church was already discernible at the end of apostolic times. Its failure was due to deviation from the true teaching of Christ, growing more and more acute among the increasing numbers of heretical sects all of whose leaders were in the power of the devil. In the third century things were worse than in the second, and from then on the downward course was relentless. In this version of history there was no place for Luther: he was to be viewed in contrast, as a single act of grace from God, a ray of eternal truth in the overwhelming darkness.

The days after Luther's death in which the author himself lived were akin to those the Church lived through immediately after the apostles had gone: Satan redoubling his assaults, striking out powerfully through the teachers of error. By the latter he meant Melanchthon, Strigel and other contemporaries. Princes and preachers must share the task of preserving the purity of doctrine from defilement and helping the Church to arise from the sickness it incurred on a diet of abuses and false doctrine. Both, princes and theologians, were answerable to the Last Judgement.

Progress, it was taken for granted, could only be negative. ' Chiefly this Church history portrays the emergence, development and profligate activities of Antichrist.'[1] It was a gloomy counterpart to Melanchthon's picture of divinely-appointed messengers repeatedly coming to the rescue of fallen man.

(a) THE WEIMAR DISPUTATION

No more precise indication of Flacius' attitude to Luther can be found than in the great *Weimar Disputation* where he met his former associate Strigel in controversy over original sin and free will. It was held in the presence of the Saxon dukes and lasted for a whole week in August 1560. The figure of the reformer looms superhuman and forbidding:

> I hear you finding fault with Luther, you who should let him lie in peace, the restorer of true religion and the singular instrument of God.

> Of course we can do nothing. It would equally have been impossible for Luther to uproot the multitude of heretical errors and papal abominations if the help of the Holy Ghost had not been granted him.

> Luther stands to accuse you of sophism, assuring us that the whole human substance is corrupt through original sin. So do I likewise, trusting in the word of God, which mentions no corrupt accident but the old man corrupt, meaning the

[1] Preface to the *Magdeburg Centurien*.

whole man, when it decrees that he drown and be re-born a new creature;—I declare it untrue that means to salvation will be found as you claim; I declare that this claim of yours is opposed to Luther and to the doctrine of our Church and to Holy Scripture.

A score of times Flacius Illyricus called upon Luther to support his theses and confound those of his opponent. As the latter based his claims on Luther too, the controversy burned hottest on the question of what Luther had really meant, Flacius frequently accusing Strigel of not understanding Luther.

The quarrel as to the authentic Luther first flared up when Melanchthon and Luther confronted one another with different versions of the doctrine of justification. It blazed fiercely in the dispute on free will and original sin known in Church history as the *Synergistic Controversy*, when for the first time real separate parties formed within the ranks of Lutheran Protestantism. Melanchthon and his supporters stressed the relative importance of personal effort in the process of salvation, maintaining that man was able to co-operate with God's grace. Matthias Flacius, heading the strict Lutherans, insisted upon the total ineptitude of man for salvation. The outcome was the compilation known as the *Weimar Book of Confutations*, 1558–59, an official condemnation of the *Confessio Augustana*, which had been largely inspired by Melanchthon and enjoyed general favour. The new Book of Confutations was sponsored by Duke Johann Friedrich von Sachsen-Weimar, strongly influenced by Flacius. Some even of the strict Lutherans took exception to it, and like Strigel became supporters of *synergism*: ' Flacius plunged into that heresy of heresies by which original sin is supposed to have become part of the substance of man through the fall of Adam.'

(b) FIRST PHASE OF LUTHERAN ORTHODOXY

Since Luther's death a new situation had arisen, or rather, an existing situation appeared in a new light after the Weimar Disputations.

In the late sixteenth century and all through the seventeenth the subject matter of theology was the proper interpretation of the Bible or the Gospel, the source from which salvation springs. Reference to Luther was final and absolute, for his doctrine and God's word were identical. But Luther was susceptible to various readings, and the theologians each claimed to be the true possessor of his meaning, treating all other interpretations with scant respect as heretical, pertaining to the devil and Antichrist.

All were convinced of the identity of Luther's message with the Gospel, and however embittered the fight, they were at one in their assurance that Luther came into the world as the messenger of God.

The novelty of the situation was evident when Flacius, basing his views on the Bible—a purely Lutheran act—instead of quoting chapter and verse, cited Luther's commentaries (chiefly on *Genesis, Psalms* and *Galatians*). This was an important precedent. The reformer had become so strongly identified with the Bible that his theology and Scripture were inseparable: at times the Bible took second place. Where Luther had used the Bible as the source of his theology, Flacius used Luther.

The narrowing of the base is evident. But the concentration of Evangelical theology and church on the reformer as the main-stay of salvation gave him that superhuman stature already noted.

All this began to take shape in the latter part of the sixteenth century.

2. GLOCCER, SPANGENBERG, SELNECCER AND OTHERS

Since the middle of the century, Catholic theology had received from the Council of Trent fresh impulse, confidence and a clear norm, and had gone over to the offensive against reformed doctrine. The latter put up a strong defence. The Catholics attacked Luther's person and his work, his supporters rallied to the rescue.

Literature on Luther, formerly bent on the pious duty of doing honour to God through the reformer and instructing the faithful, now sought cogent arguments with which to refute accusations from the Catholic side. At this time it took on a strong legendary colour and was full of anecdotes, stories and accounts of wonders and miracles.

The *Konkordienformel*, 1580, the body of Lutheran doctrine as commonly accepted, marked the passing of half a century and more since the Reformation.

The early biographies of Luther, written to honour God and instruct the faithful, lacked any real scholarly urge. This was in order, because the religious urge was strong. No one was interested in producing a piece of original work, each was content to make a compilation of well-known material for the practical purpose of instruction. Gloccer described his *Luther* as a fine selection of what Melanchthon, Mathesius and a number of other biographers had laid down ' in sizeable books on many sheets of paper.' It is precisely its lack of originality that makes his book valuable as a key to the contemporary mind.

In later sixteenth-century books about Luther, the personal touch, if it is there at all, is stereotyped and reduced to a few token traits. It was well known, and liked as a sign of Christian behaviour, that he counselled peace in political matters, deterred the Evangelical princes from plans for war, promised them God's help and protection, and made for their benefit a special selection of comforting passages from Scripture, ' so that such an one in pursuit of the enemy of the Gospel,'[1] might be provided with support and strength. From now on to the beginning of the eighteenth century, ' instrument of God,' ' chosen weapon,' were the favourite epithets, for the Reformation was a task which God ' had elected to perform by means of his chosen, constant, valiant, active and fearless instrument, Luther.'[2]

[1] Biographers of Luther of the late sixteenth century, doctors of theology under princely patronage and preachers at the Electoral courts, such as Chyträus, Selneccer and many others, cultivated a certain manner of presentation that corresponded to the German Electors' reluctance in the face of war at that time. It was greatly in the interest of these peace-seeking patrons that the reformer should be shown as the apostle of peace and preacher of obedience to secular authority. For further information on these Electors, see F. Hartung, "Der Deutsche Territorialstaat des 16. und 17. Jahrhunderts nach den fürstlichen Testamenten," in Hartung, *Volk und Staat in der Deutschen Geschichte* (1940), 94-111.

[2] Spangenberg.

Thus arose expressions such as 'the grace of God through Luther,' and 'act of benevolence to Germany from God.'[1] Biblical parallels were found for every phase of his daily life, and biblical names and titles were showered on him in utter gravity, all helping to build up the myth; he was a godly knight, a martyr, a miracle-man, a prophet, an apostle and evangelist; a Jacob, a Samson and Moses, a John and Paul. He was even the Fifth Evangelist and the Angel of the Lord.[2]

The prophet Malachias had foretold the return of Elias before the end of the world, this was fulfilled in Luther. Mathesius had described him as the best teacher, now Spangenberg described him as the best singer since apostolic times. 'Since apostolic times' became a household expression.

Luther was compared to David not only because, like the Jewish King, he composed songs to the praise and honour of God, but also, it was emphasized, because no less than in David's psalms, in Luther's songs and tunes the Holy Ghost was evident.

The old Evangelicals believed Luther was sent solely for the holy work of the Reformation, or more precisely, because God wished through Martin Luther to bring to completion the process of salvation, by restoring pure doctrine and unmasking Antichrist. Luther was called and chosen before the creation of the world 'to conduct the Lord's battle.'

Great was the act of mercy from which Luther's vocation sprang:

> How things stood in God's Church before these times is still well known. . . . The poor folk who went in error, like erring sheep with no shepherd, were taught 'devil's doctrine,' comfortless, to their everlasting harm.

---

[1] Spangenberg.

[2] To search for biblical parallels in honour of a great religious figure was a usual custom in the Middle Ages, for instance in the case of Francis and Dominic, as Clemens Bauer points out. It can be traced to the mediæval tendency to explain history theologically, that is on biblical lines. This attitude to history went on unbroken into the Reformation.

Eventually, however,

> everlasting and merciful God, Father of our Saviour Jesus
> Christ, let his wrath subside, wherewith he had properly
> punished a godless and thankless world, harkened to the pitiful
> sighing and complaining of his elect, crying out to him day
> and night, and came to their rescue: in his fathomless love and
> mercy he called up Doctor Martin Luther, of Eisleben, and
> appointed him his chosen weapon, who by the grace of God
> before all others was the first to expound the pure, true, godly
> doctrine aright, as it is contained in Holy Scripture, and bring
> it into the light of day.[1]

Luther's divine mission, a matter of faith, was now to be
proved by reference to the Bible and Church history. Reformation theologians were fond of working on the pragmatic proof
ex eventu. There was the visible success of the Evangelical cause:
their conclusions pointed to the invisible author. Thus, Luther
preached

> with intelligence, courage and constancy (however bitter the
> occasion might be and often had to endure temptations, bitter
> sweats and agonies from the devil, in great danger of his very
> life)—it is impossible that such work could have reached such
> dimensions by means of merely human power or wisdom,
> however exalted: a sure sign that God ruled and guided this
> man through his Holy Spirit and bestowed on his calling and
> office divine prosperity and blessing.[1]

A truly mediæval naïveté was the mark of this pragmatic
attempt to recognize the finger of God in each single event of
the Reformation. David Chyträus believed that the Emperor
Charles V became involved in his French wars between 1521
and 1529 ' through a special provision of God,' so that in his
absence the Edict of Worms could be carried through unhindered
' and the doctrine of the Gospel be planted and spread more
surely and more widely in Germany and other lands.'
    The same naïveté coloured the proofs from Church history

[1] Gloccer.

which were submitted in all seriousness. The irrefutable conclusion was drawn from remarks by Augustine, Catherine of Siena, Huss, Johann Wessel and others, ' that the counsel and design of God had to endure and be fulfilled; that is, that the Church of God had to be cleansed of the pharasaical papal leaven, wherefore God elected to use Dr. Luther.' Holy Scripture itself was required to show the divine origin of Luther's activities. . . . Actually of course, in so far as they are not foretelling the Messias, the prophetic passages of Holy Scripture refer to the end of the world and all that goes with it: perplexity and horror among nations and realms, and to the Last Judgement and the ' new heaven and new earth ' beyond. This the Reformation theologians knew very well, and they were disposed to see their own time as no ordinary period of history but the last stretch of time immediately before the end. They were convinced in all faith that they stood on the brink of the end of the world.

Another tradition grew up, based on the prophet Malachias: ' Behold I will send you Elias the prophet before the coming of the great and dreadful day of the Lord.'[1] Luther was of course Elias. All these tendencies met in the Lutheran apocalypse, with Luther the revealer of Antichrist as centre-piece. Before the end of the century the Antichrist doctrine was being taught in the schools as a proof of the divine nature of Luther's mission.

There were as a matter of fact two Antichrists: one was the Turk, Gog and Magog;—' the other shall reign in the temple of God,' that is to say he was the pope. To unmask the pope was a Christian act, an act of God's mercy, it freed Christendom from the domination of the devil. And the man who did it was

---

[1] *Mal.* iv, 5. The idea was put into verse by Nicolaus Hermann and included in the Evangelical Hymn-book:

> *Elias vor dem Jüngsten Tag*
> *soll wiederkommen auf Erden,*
> *dass er der bösen Welt absag,*
> *dass Christus kommen werde.*
> *Aber der teure Gottesmann*
> *hat sich längst hören und sehen lahn;*
> *drum ist das End nicht ferne.*

' the beloved highly-enlightened man Dr. Martin Luther in the year of Christ 1517 above all.' Thus Luther's act was tantamount to an act of God, for which he had merely selected Luther and ' armed him with the Holy Ghost.' Therefore Luther was sent from God.

In one of his hymns Luther called the foes of Christ by name: praying for the downfall and death of pope and Turk, who seek to drive Christ from his throne:

> *Erhalt uns, Herr, bei deinem Wort*
> *und steur des Papsts und Türken Mord,*
> *die Jesum Christum, deinem Sohn,*
> *stürzen wollen von seinem Thron.*

As time went on, the sharp outline became blurred, the inconsistencies came to light, and towards the end of the century the Evangelical theologians, though using the same terms to describe their opponents, had shifted their position considerably. ' Pure Christian doctrine' stood on narrower ground, the adversary had prospered and multiplied.

Luther had had to defend himself against enemies from all sides, each claiming, as he did himself, support in Holy Scripture: papists, anabaptists, sacramentalists, antinomists, and ' more than thirty public and secret heretics.'[1] But the theological schools that came after had many more: to those recognized by the Reformation as foes were to be added as ' seducers,' all those Lutherans who had gone off the prescribed lines.

So Luther was reduced to a special form of Lutheranism. In all schools of theology his doctrine, as the pure word of God, was held in high estimation. This at least meant a common line, which, in spite of the divisions which occurred towards the end of the century, culminated in seventeenth-century orthodoxy.

A coin minted by the Elector of Brandenburg, Joachim II, dated 1564, bears this motto:

> *Gottes Wort und Luthers Lehr*
> *wird vergehen nimmermehr.*[2]

[1] Selneccer.
[2] God's word and Luther's doctrine will never pass away.

Nicolaus Selneccer engraved the couplet:

> *Was Lutherus einmal gelehrt,*
> *bei dem bleiben wir unverkehrt.*[1]

And Georg Gloccer in a long poem let Luther speak for himself:

> *Der Jüngste Tag wird kommen bald,*
> *da wird Gott wecken Jung und Alt,*
> *Nach seinem Wort und meiner Lehr*
> *Gott richten wird in aller Ehr.*[2]

Clearly it crossed no one's mind to criticize Luther, he was with his doctrine set on a pedestal and worshipped ' in holiness and in the mystery of God.' It was no longer possible to draw from the source the reformer had drawn from, but only to take what he gave, scorning all that had not passed through his hands. The Evangelical *Konkordienbuch*, commissioned by the Evangelical princes and completed after painstaking preparatory work by different theologians in 1580, was intended to unite the various Lutheran schools of theology and provide them with a common base. Alongside the three old Christian creeds (the Apostles', the Nicean and the Athanasian) it offered the two catechisms of Luther, his *Schmalkaldischen* Article (a dogmatic statement setting out the Evangelical case against the Council of Trent—1537), and the *Augsburg Confession*, as official Evangelical articles of faith with validity as dogma.

3. SUMMARY—THE SIXTEENTH CENTURY

Remember that the meaning of history was not *in* history but *beyond* it, in the invisible but ever-present reality of God.

History seen as the history of redemption and salvation unfolded an imposing perspective of events from Adam onwards.

This view dominated the whole period, and the Reformation saw itself as the restoration of the old invisible spiritual Church

---

[1] What Luther once taught we will abide by without reversal.

[2] The last day will soon be here when God will waken young and old. God will judge in all honour according to his word and my doctrine.

as it should be, the original Christian community built on love and the pure true teaching of Christ; also as a freeing of Christendom from the bonds of Satan—for which effusive words of thanksgiving were found. There was no doubt at all but that the renewal of Church life was a blessing of no common sort; all good gifts come from the Father of Light,[1] and the Reformation was from him too.

It is important to realize the rôle of Luther, the man chosen by God as his instrument to renew the Church, through whom the salvation of Christendom was effected.

Justification by faith was for Luther a personal experience, which he was driven by conscience to publish. His followers seized upon the principle, expanded it into a doctrine, and imposed on the faithful literal acceptance: living experience became dogmatic theology. This is the difference between Luther and Lutheranism.

But the freedom of decision according to conscience which Luther had claimed as his right was categorically denied to the old Protestants by Lutheranism. In the biographies, speeches and sermons, there is after 1546 no mention of conscience, but instead a strong emphasis on doctrine.

A little later, after Mathesius and Sleidan, Luther was left with a stereotyped set of accessories and was as irrevocably committed to them as St. Catherine to her wheel or St. George to his dragon. He lost his individuality and towered into superhuman and mythical regions. The whole greatness of the Reformation was reflected back on him.

In the course of the controversies, a main part of his doctrine hardened into dogma. The effort to create a comprehensive system gave birth to that Evangelical orthodoxy which dominated the seventeenth century but was already in existence at the end of the sixteenth.

A remarkable transformation had taken place in little over half a century. In 1520–30 Luther was the great contemporary who valiantly declared war on Church abuses, and whom deep faith and the study of theology urged on to purify Christian

[1] James i, 17.

HANS SACHS

MELANCHTHON

doctrine, renew the Church and preach living spiritual Christianity with zeal and fervour. By 1580–90 he had become a father of the Church, honoured practically as the founder of a religion, inspired by the Holy Ghost, from whose doctrine no deviation was allowed; a teacher and prophet dispensing dogma.

What Luther taught was entitled to the same observance as the word of God, and any other opinion was to be rooted out as error. His authority replaced the authority of the Bible: Luther based his claims on Holy Scripture and Lutherans based theirs on the reformer. In brief, after the Reformation period proper he ceased to be regarded as a man and became a compendium of saving truth and right thinking.

CHAPTER III

THE SEVENTEENTH CENTURY: THE ORTHODOX ATTITUDE

1. INSCRIPTIONS AND PRESCRIPTIONS

THE part of Germany that owed allegiance to the *Augsburg Confession* continued the work of building up a body of orthodox doctrine on the foundations laid in the sixteenth century. As we saw, Luther's doctrine was the *orthodoxia*, the true Christian doctrine necessary to salvation. The faithful were connected with Luther not so much historically as by a bond of living faith. There was practically no interest in the Reformation as such, all important was the truth of the faith. Luther was not studied but simply believed in. He was the concern of theology, not history.

The jubilee of the posting of the theses in Wittenberg in 1617 and of the *Confessio Augustana* in 1630 was each time the occasion for public declarations on the part of the authorities. Jubilees as understood in the nineteenth and twentieth centuries they certainly were not: they were celebrated like holy days, like Christmas and Easter. In many Evangelical provinces and cities special coins were struck, some bearing the inscription:

Verbum Domini manet in æternum

The inscriptions on the 1617 coins were stylized. A coin of Duke Philip II of Pomerania shows Samson breaking the jaw of a lion, and the inscription runs:

Obturavit os leonis, 1517.

The lion was the pope, Samson was Luther.

A coin of the Saxon Elector was inscribed:

D.(eo) S.(oli) G.(loria) Jubilæus primus reformati per D. Lutheru(m) papatus.[1]

[1] To God alone the glory. First jubilee of the papacy reformed by Dr. Luther.

A Strasbourg coin was inscribed:

> *Pro religionis centum ante annos*
> *divinitus restitutæ memoria.*[1]

Another coin amplified this text:

> *Memoria jubilæi primi ob divinitus restitutam*
> *per D. Martinum Lutherum religionem Christianam.*[2]

A Saxon coin named the century 1517-1617:

> *Seculum Lutheranum.*

On another the reformer was called:

> *Mart. Luther: Elias ultimi seculi*

and the main article of faith of the orthodox is engraved on a memorial coin of the year 1617:

> *Gottes Wort ist Luthers Lehr,*
> *darum vergeht sie nimmerm [ehr].*[3]

A similar coin was struck in 1655 to celebrate the centenary of the Augsburg agreement of 1555 (by which the Lutherans obtained from the State a decree that subjects were to submit to the religion of the reigning prince or move to another province):

> *Confessio nostra triumphat—Usque Dei*
> *verbum manet et doctrina Lutheri . . .*[4]

The common picture in men's minds was of Luther as restorer of Church and religion, whose doctrine was Gospel truth. This picture was officially sponsored.

Moreover the restorer of the Church was foretold in biblical prophecy, which gave added sanction to the instructions which the Elector Johann Georg of Saxony drew up for the proper celebration of the Reformation centenary (Dresden, August 12, 1617). He ordained Church services to last eight days, from

[1] In memory of the restoration of religion by God a hundred years ago.

[2] In memory of the first jubilee of God's restoration of Christian religion through Doctor Martin Luther.

[3] God's word is Luther's doctrine, which shall therefore never pass away.

[4] Our faith is triumphant—The word of God and Luther's doctrine remain for ever.

October 26 to November 2, and himself provided the themes on which the sermons were to be preached. For October 31, he wrote: ' In the place of the Gospel read *Daniel* xii ' (=*Daniel* xi, 36–45). His introductory commentary runs:

> . . . Daniel clearly predicts Antichrist, depicted by the Holy Ghost in the person of the king, that is: the pope, acting and behaving after his own inclination, who raises himself above all that God is and stands for, in utter disregard of honourable love for women and God; who honours a mass-idol (called Maozim) as his god, and seduces many people with extensive presents;—and predicts also how the Almighty in his own time will strike fear into him, with a loud cry from morning till midnight, as indeed did occur through the beloved man and instrument of God, Dr. Luther of blessed memory, a hundred years ago.

Then followed the reading of the passage.

The order of service for November 1 was prescribed in the same way. Instead of the Gospel, the fourteenth chapter of the *Revelation of St. John* was to be read,

> in which the Holy Ghost plainly predicts how in the latter days, when Antichrist will for a time be made strong and powerful, the Almighty will send an angel: that is, a blessed teacher, preacher and reformer, who is to proclaim the Gospel to all nations and by means of his preaching to overthrow the great city of Babylon, that is: the Roman papacy . . . all of which in the last hundred years was fulfilled through Dr. Luther of blessed memory and his true followers, the Evangelical theologians, teachers and preachers in many king- doms, principalities and electorates, provinces and dominions, and above all throughout Germany.

It is clear that the charge to preachers to interpret Luther according to certain tenets was one which the civic authorities were empowered to enforce.

2. LUTHER AND LUTHERAN ORTHODOXY

If Luther's doctrine, office and appointment were not of God, then, it was pointed out, everything else connected with Luther was untenable. On the other hand, if Luther's appointment and office can be proved to be from God, then all attacks on his human frailty are without force. The question was a vital one in the seventeenth century and lay at the very heart of the theological controversy between Evangelicals and Catholics. The Evangelical side swore by Luther's divine appointment, the Reformation was to them an act of God, Luther merely carrying it out. The Catholics contested this claim as incompatible with their conception of Church and hierarchy, council and dogma. The Tridentine Council had declared invalid the very basis of Lutheran theology —the article on justification by faith alone—and could not admit that the author, who had built up a new church upon it, was in possession of a divine appointment.[1]

In the course of the contest each side sought to loosen cornerstones in the edifice of the other, in order to bring the whole structure down at a stroke. On the Catholic side such a stone was the dogma of the divine foundation of the papacy; on the Lutheran side, the doctrine of the divine appointment of Luther.

(a) JOHANN GERHARD

Johann Gerhard entered the fray with a special Disputation in support of Luther's divine appointment.

The exaggerated claims made for Luther as prophet, apostle, fifth evangelist and one inspired by the Holy Ghost were hotly contested by Catholic (mainly Jesuit) theologians, and with some measure of success, with the result that the Protestants toned them down somewhat. But theological proof was all the more urgently needed for the claim that Luther, if not under the direct inspiration of the Holy Ghost, at least owed his doctrine and Reformation to God, and to supply such proof was one of

[1] The Tridentine Council laid down that justification is brought about by the grace of God working together with man's good will, and condemned the Lutheran doctrine which excluded good will.

the most formidable tasks to which Lutheran dogmatic theology applied itself.

Here was work for scholars, and there ensued a marked decrease in the crude accusations of heresy and the highly-coloured glorification of their hero which disfigured popular Lutheran literature. The tone improved, the expression grew more prudent; effort was concentrated on consolidating the theological position so that the opponent would have to treat it with respect.

Exactly one hundred years after the posting of the theses in Wittenberg, Johann Gerhard held his Disputation on 'the legitimate appointment of blessed Luther to his office and to the Reformation.' His point of departure was the objections raised by the famous Jesuit theologians, Becanus and Cardinal Bellarmine. He rallied arguments of his own in support of an indirect legitimate appointment and direct extraordinary gifts, and finally refuted one of the Catholic objections. He very earnestly considered the question of how far Luther had had the right to reform the Church.

Formerly it was proof sufficient to show how Luther's doctrine agreed with the Gospel. The novelty in Gerhard's approach lay in his preliminary suggestion that the two questions, legitimacy of appointment and truth of doctrine, should be kept apart. For

a man may be legitimately appointed and yet teach wrongfully and heretically. . . . On the other hand he may teach the truth and yet lack legitimate appointment. Therefore if Luther was not legitimately appointed we can by no means draw the consequences that his doctrine is on that account false and erroneous.

Then came a painstaking deployment of arguments in the course of which this able Lutheran theologian set Lutheranism within very stringent bounds. Not even the most explicit of Luther's utterances could be traced to divine revelation. If Luther was firmly convinced of the truth of his own doctrine, it was not on this account either a revelation or a substitute for a legitimate appointment.

It was Bellarmine who provoked such dotting of the i's. Gerhard began by quoting him:

> Whoever is sent to preach will either be sent by God through ordinary ecclesiastical authority, or will as something extraordinary be sent by God alone. Whoever is appointed by ordinary ecclesiastical authority must be able to show the certificate of Ordination by the Bishop, usually a document with a seal attached. Whoever is sent from God alone must show forth the *sigillum Dei*: the seal of God, in other words, a miracle.

Whereupon Gerhard considerably reduced the claims for marks of the supernatural, formerly so readily attributed to the reformer. But he insisted that Luther's appointment to office in the Church had taken the usual course and had occurred directly: in 1507 Luther was ordained priest and given authority to teach the word of God; in 1508 he was appointed, by deed of his lord the Elector Frederick the Wise and of his superior Johann von Staupitz, university professor and priest to the parish church in Wittenberg, an appointment which laid on him the duty to expound the law and preach the book of life. In 1512, with his doctor's degree, he was granted power ' to defend the truth of heavenly doctrine against all other faiths, of whatever sort, by means of the spoken and written word.'

But all this, said Gerhard, was still insufficient to empower Luther to undertake the reformation of the Church.

The fining down of his supernatural character was not carried to such lengths that it left no room for the play of gifts and idiosyncrasies with which Luther was so richly endowed. If they did not warrant his promotion to the rank of an apostle, they placed him far above a usual normal vocation to Church service. Without raising the status of his office, they did adorn it most singularly.

> It must not and cannot be denied that in his ecclesiastical office and in his regular professional duties and in all that concerns the carrying through of the Reformation and the attack on the kingdom of Antichrist, something extraordinary and special was at work, which, if it cannot exactly all along

the line be called a direct appointment, completely out of the ordinary as the Apostles' was, yet causes him to soar house-high above the common run of servants of the Church. It is, according to D. Hunnius, the *heroica pars* of his vocation.

Unique in Luther was the combination of an ordinary appointment and extraordinary gifts. It was the latter which gave him the capacity to reform the Church. Gerhard drew up a systematic catalogue of extraordinary gifts.

This catalogue, which is called *extraordinarium et peculiare*, included without distinction personal characteristics (such as Luther's knowledge of Scripture and his courage) and external events (for instance the success of the Reformation). Whether personal or external, the items were selected not for their own sakes but as signs of God's action. Such a catalogue was a commonplace. Gerhard's is noteworthy, however, because of the ingenious way he applied the various headings to his main theme.

Naturally Gerhard's thesis was rejected by the Catholics. He knew it would be, and in claiming that Luther incontestably possessed a divine appointment, he knew he was to all intents and purposes rejecting the Roman Church as such, in so far as its principles and dogmas were opposed to Luther.

It belonged deeply and organically to the Lutheran creed to condemn Catholicism, it was of necessity the reverse side of adherence to the creed. Negatively a matter of blind inter-confessional hatred, positively it appeared as a stand for the pure word of God. The Lutheran church service included a brand-marking of all who treated the Gospel with contempt (first and foremost the head and members of the Roman Church). The Catholic form of worship was rejected. This was, moreover, an act of self-preservation, for the existence of the old Church places a question-mark against the claim of any other to be the true Church of Christ. If Lutheranism wanted to prove it was, it had to prove that Catholicism was *not* the true community which held fast to the word. Johann Gerhard with his considered factual approach served his cause far better than the more passionate attacks of other Lutherans.

The controversy of Gerhard with Becanus, the Jesuit theologian, is important too.

In 1616, in his Viennese disputation, *de vocatione ministrorum*, Becanus stated:

> Luther was not appointed and sent in the proper sense of these terms, for he was not given power and jurisdiction (to carry out the Reformation). Though he was ordained to the priesthood by a Catholic bishop and received from him power to perform the consecration of the Eucharist at Mass, he received from the bishop neither power nor jurisdiction to reform religion and the state of the Church, nor to attack Catholic doctrine in Saxony and its neighbouring provinces. Nor was his a direct appointment and mission from God.

Becanus elaborated his theme with examples, of which we will cite two as reported by Gerhard:

> What Luther said to the people was full of lies, errors and falsifications.
>
> Luther states himself: ' Nothing is to be believed that is not in God's word.' But nowhere in God's word is it written that Luther was sent to reform the Church.

To the first Gerhard answered, as one sure of his case, that an accusation was no proof, and if it could be proved that Luther's writings were full of lies, errors and falsifications, then he was indeed no true prophet.

In reply to the second he mustered the familiar arguments of the Luther-allegory based on biblical prophecy.

He met the accusation that Luther had no charge to carry out the Reformation by lending to the terms *potestas, iurisdictio,* and *catholica doctrina* a meaning far less precise than their usual definition in the Catholic sense. Spilling out the content of fundamental Catholic ideas, he achieved the feat of apparently turning the Catholic Church against its own doctrine. The basic belief of Lutheranism being that Luther's doctrine is identical with God's word, in reverse it reads: God's word and papal doctrine are *not* the same.

When Luther obtained his doctor's degree he had to swear an oath that ' he would not teach untrue and strange doctrine condemned by the Church and offensive to pious ears.' Later in the course of the theological controversies the question often arose whether Luther had broken his oath. The Protestants answered: No, for he was empowered by this oath to combat superstition and error and his reformation showed that he had done so. On the contrary, said the Catholics, he has broken his oath for ' it was taken as covering not only Holy Scripture but also the Church, that is the papal *decreta*.' Gerhard replied: ' He swore to the *decreta* only on condition that they tallied with God's word. When he later discovered that they deviated from Christ's own teaching, he denounced them with full authority.'

These last words reveal how an entirely new conception of the Church had grown up, a strictly non-Catholic one. In short, legality for Luther's church could only be claimed by men who no longer knew what a church stood for in the strongly legalistic Catholic definition. The orthodox Lutherans' idea was general and non-juridical. Laymen in the persons of the civic authorities had a considerable say in it. Gerhard set out to define what it was.

> Concerning the Reformation [he said], two things must be taken into account. First, the confutation of error; secondly, the abolition of idolatry.
>
> The confutation of error is the concern of the Church. But the open abolition of idolatry is a paramount duty of the Christian lay authority. On the example of the pious kings of the old covenant, who swept away the service of Baal, it must effect pious reforms in conjunction with the Church and must set up an unadulterated church service (meaning a regular order of church service in each province), especially when the bishops are found to take too little interest in their office.

Gerhard called the Church as a whole

> a community of people gathered together and called out of the world into the kingdom of God through preaching of the word and dispensing of the sacraments, in which are found

the elect, as fore-known (*prænotio*) to the Father, those who truly and perseveringly are believers in Christ, along with others, no saints but acknowledging the same faith.

Elsewhere Gerhard set to work to define the ' true Church ' and to prove it to be the Lutheran:

Whichever Church has unadulterated preaching of the word and legitimate dispensation of the sacraments is the true, genuine orthodox Church; but the Lutheran Church (rightly so-called by us) has unadulterated preaching of the word and legitimate dispensation of the sacraments. Therefore the Lutheran Church is the true, genuine and orthodox Church.

Lutheran doctrine and God's word being identical—and we have seen this was a first principle for Gerhard—the fact of the Reformation and the existence of the Evangelical Church had sufficient legitimization. But to cease to believe in this identification was to cause the whole structure to totter, for it stood by that and nothing else.

Moreover, it was un-Lutheran to make Evangelical Christianity depend a hundred per cent on the ' doctrine ' of justification by faith and bind conscience to the letter of this doctrine, if at the same time no room was left for the very principle of the Reformation itself out of which the new faith was born: freedom of conscience independent of all human authority, bound to the authority of the Bible alone. A movement arose in course of time in defence of this principle, and at the turn of the eighteenth century shook the whole structure of orthodox Lutheranism.

Before turning to the new movement, called pietism, let us recapitulate the main points of Lutheran orthodoxy.

(b) RECAPITULATION

I. There were in the main two motives for writing about Luther: the need to answer attacks from Catholic controversial theology, when the tension between the two camps was so agonizingly painful that each laboured under a tremendous propulsion to review its spiritual foundations; and there was the trust to keep the memory of Luther fresh and preserve the purity of his doctrine. ' I should like to revive his blessed memory which has almost faded away due to the inclemency of the time.'[1] This was seen simply as a service to religious truth. But such was the concentration on doctrine that Luther's own abundant and varied writings were hardly read at all in the seventeenth century—not even the smaller catechism, says Seckendorf.

II. Luther's many-sided personality was concealed behind his doctrine and this was due to the fact that Luther was considered in a purely religious light, that is as preacher and propounder, and what he propounded was ' the pure doctrine of Jesus Christ.' That was all. It is impossible to emphasize too strongly the subordination of Luther to his doctrine, at this period.

The orthodox preachers of the seventeenth century are full of this theme. ' We hold by what he teaches from the word of God and take no notice of his person.'[2] For

we know from God's word that we should not turn our attention to the teacher as a person but consider only the thing taught, whether it be or not God's word. That Judas betrayed, that Peter denied the Lord Christ, that Thomas fell into great disbelief, that Paul was a great persecutor of Christianity, that Peter and Paul quarrelled, does not detract from their teaching; if an angel even came from heaven and preached falsely, his doctrine would be no better for the fact. Yea, when a prophet prophesies, and performs miracles and signs, it is of no avail, if he teach against the word of God. Therefore a great and good person cannot make doctrine good when it is false and a small and bad person cannot make doctrine false and bad in itself when it is right. Therefore we were not obliged to trouble ourselves about the person of Luther or to answer accusations against that person, as long as his doctrine is right and in conformity with scripture.[2]

---

[1] Dannhauer.   [2] Müller.

III. Luther was not a subject of historical research but an object of faith.

This relieved the Lutherans of the necessity to refute in detail Catholic accusations finding fault with Luther's personality and its weaknesses. Lutheranism did not take such attacks as a serious threat to its existence.

IV. Such a view of Luther is one-sided of course and misses a lot, but it is deeply religious and probably, for all its one-sidedness, comes nearer to Luther than the whole body of modern research with its wide knowledge of sources and its clever application of historical and psychological methods. The seventeenth-century view was still in an unbroken line with that of the Reformation period itself. Reading the Evangelical writers of the seventeenth century, we gain real insight into what Luther meant to his church in the first century and a half after its foundation. He was their great pastor, father and teacher. Not only in matters of religious feeling but also, and above all, in matters of faith and dogma. The Protestants of the Reformation period, and those of the Baroque period that followed, the time of absolutism and the divine right of kings, were people who really were at home in a Christian world order, an order where it was taken for granted that Jesus Christ, with God the Father, was entitled to claim dominion over the whole life of the individual and of the community, God and eternal life were no empty words but *mysteria tremenda*, facts with which each single man was directly confronted. One need only read such passages as the hymn of the Hambourg Pastor Johann Rist (1607–1667), ' *O Ewigkeit, du Donnerswort* ' (Eternity, thou thunderous word), to become aware of the immense tension in the existence of those men with their sense of the eternal impinging on their lives. It was men of this sort who turned to Luther for instruction as to how to behave in order to be with God in all eternity. For the sake of these things his memory was cherished.

V. The belief in the Reformation as a supernatural act of supreme importance in the history of salvation, and the intolerance with which all rival interpretations of Luther were regarded, were both greatly strengthened in their hold on men's

minds by the possibility lapse of time had provided of an historical
approach: the argument for the supernatural nature of the
Reformation was drawn from its successful development as an
historical fact.

The Antichrist theology of the Reformation passed practically
unchanged into the seventeenth century. That the pope was now
considered worse than Mohammed and more godless than the
Turk was supererogatory. The negative side of the Reformation,
the destruction of the kingdom of Antichrist, could be seen to
have gone so far that in many parts of the world the very name
of pope had disappeared.[1] The devil retained his importance: he
was still the power which, being most badly hit by the
Reformation, most strove to undo it and to this end favoured
wrong doctrine and the growth of sects. The positive side of the
Reformation was the return of the Church to its proper form.
Its medium was the preaching of the Gospel. The Reformation
was in fact simply ' the improvement of doctrine and public
service of God, both of which had suffered in the course of time;
and far more effective than any improvement brought about at
any time by rulers of this world.' And apart from right doctrine
and the revealing of Antichrist, what was most notable was the
conversio solemnis, magna, admiranda, ' the conversion worthy of
all admiration, great, most conducive to holiness of whole
kingdoms, peoples and states and their return from the new
gods to the old God the Father and to the true old wholesome
apostolic faith.'

A favourite theme was to compare the Reformation to
apostolic times. That too came out of the sixteenth century, but
it was done minutely and boldly, parallels being found where
the facts could not really be said to tally. When Johannes Müller
wrote that Lutheran preaching had had the effect of persuading
the ' cloister-virgins ' that their state was no holier than that of
other people, he added gratuitously that this was a miracle of
the same rank as the conversion of the Jewish and heathen world
after the Resurrection and Ascension of Christ.

The return of the Church to its proper way of life was the

[1] Dannhauer.

real achievement of the Reformation: a godly work. But it was natural to the rationalizing faith of the period to seek proofs, and this proof-seeking usually went round in circles, which is a sign that conviction tended to be stronger than logic. One assumed what had to be proved, that is, the identity of God's word with Luther's doctrine, and the proof worked like this: as the doctrine is the word of God, therefore the Reformation is a godly work. And by analogy; as the disclosure and overthrow of Antichrist could only be a godly work, therefore the Reformation, which undertook both, is one too. The same conclusion could be reached with almost any set of facts, for instance, ' the fortunate and marvellous outcome of the Reformation,' ' the marvellous preservation of Luther in fighting his foes,' ' his excellent and powerful talents.' Finally even the papists were called upon to provide evidence:

> They no longer preach to fishes and birds, midges and flies are no longer excommunicated, the swine of St. Antony are no longer fattened, the Poltergeists come less often: these and other things of the kind the papists have wisely put an end to, and thus of necessity witness that Dr. Luther's reformation was right and godly.[1]

However childish this may seem, behind it all there was a purely religious estimation of the Reformation as such.

VI. The same explanation holds for the marked intolerance of the seventeenth century. Friedrich Wilhelm, the great Elector of Brandenburg (1640–88), arranged a debate on religion between the two Protestant confessions. It took place in Berlin in 1662–63.

The reformed party (Calvinists) expressed itself thus:

> Of Luther we hold as of other men, that he was compound of flesh and spirit, and that of no mean quality—*nihil mediocre*. When spirit had the upper hand, then he showed *heroicos motus*; when however flesh ruled, he broke out in horrid *paradoxa*, which we *tanquam verenda patris ecclesia* will gladly leave covered over, as long as we are not required to lay some part of it bare

[1] Müller.

—a reasonably sensible remark, in retort to which Paul Gerhardt, at that time Lutheran provost in Berlin, rose in wrath: ' there was no occasion to scold and misrepresent poor Luther. It was clear how fond the Calvinists really were of blessed Luther.'

As is known, the debate reached no agreement. Paul Gerhardt renounced his pastoral office rather than make the slightest concession. All that was asked was the signing of a statement that the two parties were prepared to tolerate and respect each other as Christian confessions. But it was too much for the strict Lutherans. They would not even admit the possibility that the Calvinists with their Calvinistic faith could attain to salvation. It was sheer stubborn dogmatic intolerance, coming from the heart of the conviction that their Lutheran doctrine contained the whole of apostolic Christianity, and that it was nothing new but the old true doctrine, and moreover that their communion was the old true Church and no new one, and finally that all deviation was the work of the devil.

Thus the Lutherans with their strict dogma flocked round Luther as the very source of salvation. Their manner of honouring him lacked independence but was genuine and vital whether they were defending him or of their own accord broke out in praise of him, or fell to contemplating his shadow on the things of this world, the last word was always praise, glory, gratitude. And it is this which really gives the best impression of orthodox Lutheranism: how it was possessed of the spirit of Luther. It is a key to the general spiritual condition of the time.

VII. It was a stern and narrow faith, and we may easily overlook the fact that the men who clung to it also made themselves very much at home in the world. But contemporary reports witness how stubborn dogmatic strictness and a healthy enjoyment of life could exist side by side combined with downright pleasure in worldly success. This may not have been the general rule, but it occurred and deserves mention. A powerful grasp of sensual as well as spiritual matters is a hall-mark of the Baroque period, and this coincides largely with the period of dogmatic controversy. Johannes Müller wrote an introduction to his *Lutherus defensus* (1634–1645) which reveals something of

GOTTFRIED WILHELM LEIBNIZ

PHILIPP JACOB SPENER

the lively worldly interests of the seventeenth century. There exist more characteristic examples of Baroque vitality, with its heavenly and earthly aspirations, but it serves our purpose:

God almighty has blessed this city of Hamburg with very great benefits on behalf of many other cities in Germany. For whoever shall think upon the size of the city within its walls, the strong and cunning fortifications, the great number of inhabitants, the sundry nationalities and foreign peoples who partly live here, partly travel away or return day by day, the open passage to the sea for ships, the admiralty and the good administration of the sailings; the great body of merchants, the trade and traffic, the precious fruits and vegetables and other wares which are brought here in large quantities from Holland, England, France, Italy, Spain, Turkey, Barbary, Egypt, India and other kingdoms and countries; the lovely prospect of this city, which lies amid fruitful fields between two waterways, the Elbe and the Elster; the well-built summer-houses and valuable gardens; the handsome citizens and the great gathering of learned, wise, and famous people both in and out of the Council; the abundant daily provision of all the requirements of life; the neighbourhood of many distinguished cities, the well-built finely-decorated churches; the admirable ordering of prisons, orphanages and hostelries as well as of other public institutions; the prosperity of the inhabitants; the openings for all sorts of artists, craftsmen, and officials; the citizens' excellent arrangements for the maintenance of law and order, in peace and war, and many other benefits of God: to think upon all this is to recognize indeed that the paths of the All-Highest drop fatness[1] and of this city might well be said what was once written of the plain of Jordan, that it was even as the garden of the Lord.[2]

But of all the benefits of God the greatest is, that merciful God gave us in this place for our salvation his Holy Word. In church and school there was pure clear preaching in the

---

[1] *Psalm* lxv, 11 A.V.   [2] *Genesis* xiii, 10.

time of Charlemagne (801) when Saxony was converted to Christianity and the arch-abbey of Hambourg was built. But through the wickedness of the devil and the corruption of the papists, religion later became darkened and Holy Scripture was suppressed. But Almighty God has at last through his grace had mercy upon this city and let the light of his Gospel spring up and shine forth. For when Dr. Martin Luther, urged and assisted by the Holy Ghost, rose against papist errors, so also in the year 1521 a pious conscientious preacher was found, one Master Otto Stiefel, Pastor at St. Catherine's Church. . . .

PART II

TRANSITION PERIOD AROUND 1700
FIRST REACTION AGAINST STRICT CONFESSIONALISM

CHAPTER I
VEIT VON SECKENDORF

TOWARDS the end of the seventeenth century a very exhaustive history of Lutheranism was published, the reply of an Evangelical layman to two French accounts of the history of the Reformation, one by Bossuet, Bishop of Meaux, the other by the Jesuit Maimbourg. The author was for many years an official at the court of Duke Ernst the Pious of Gotha (1640–75) and had made himself a name with his book on the German principality state (1655). For a short time towards the end of his life and century, he held the appointment of Chancellor of the newly-founded university of Halle. His name was Veit Ludwig Freiherr von Seckendorf (1626–92).

His *Historia Lutheranismi* seems, for all its astounding comprehensiveness, to have been a popular book. It appeared first in 1692 and in a second edition in 1694. The sub-title ran ' *Commentarius historicus et apologeticus de Lutheranismo sive de religionis reformatione ductu D. Martini Lutheri . . .*', indicating that it was written to defend the Reformation as an historical fact. Apart from defensive action under Catholic fire, its motive was to safeguard and perpetuate the memory of the Reformation. There was nothing disquieting about that. Nonetheless, and simply by keeping steadily to the task he had set himself, the author found himself exploring ground that lay beyond the normal scope of strict Lutheranism. He was deeply convinced of the truth of the orthodox Lutheran faith. In his religious attitude he belonged to his time, in that his whole life was lived within the setting of his faith. But other forces were alive in him with which orthodoxy had not as yet come to terms. A religious impulse underlay his historical work:

> The prince often discussed with me the possibility of writing down the history of the Reformation which took place in the past century in Germany and particularly in

Saxony. A theme of high utility and honour was offered, I was to essay to bring to light, from material in the archives of the principalities and cities and those in private ownership, why the reformation of religion took place and with what success, and how from small beginnings it achieved its present state which the world never ceases to wonder at. ' God's finger,' he said, ' was certainly at work. It is sheer ingratitude not to recognize it and not conscientiously to safeguard and perpetuate the memory of such great events.' . . . I undertook the work of putting it down on paper with the assurance I was writing for my own benefit too, and that I was making more and more progress in the knowledge of both historical and dogmatic truth.

1. ORTHODOXY LOOSENS ITS HOLD

It was clearly not Seckendorf's intention to alter the commonly accepted view of Luther. But in fact he did so. The reformer lost his byzantine majesty and rigidity and became human again. He was still as chief actor firmly implicated in the events of the Reformation, seen as ' God's finger,' but Martin Luther was no longer simply the instrument of divine activity, a living man was disclosed, with all his warmth, vigour, passions. ' I have described this Luther's beginnings, his studies and his daily life, without either belittling his God-given gifts or attributing to him more than his due. I can state that his doctrine was not a sudden inspiration, but grew out of steady meditation and improved with time.' The first seven years of the Reformation seemed to the author wonderful: a time of ferment and increase, of fresh living growth—better than the later years of the consolidation of Church and dogma. And the early years he called the *propria historia Lutheri*, the real history of Luther. He explored both periods thoroughly for he feared his sheer enthusiasm for the earlier time might offend one or another of his readers. He was attracted by what was humanly striking in Luther's personal achievement: his courage and his endurance in a time when he lacked all human protection; his fearlessness in the midst of the dangers with which his numerous enemies threatened him; his superhuman capacity for work, in spite of poor health and meagre nourishment: taken all in all, it was a miracle that the man could endure one year's life at this pitch, let alone seven. ' At that time the Lutheran Evangelium struck like lightning to all the ends of Europe almost, bereft of princely patronage, and with no support from external powers, borne aloft by sheer force of conviction.' How important this was for Seckendorf appears in the following passage:

> Thus, when we consider the inner drive rather than the outward success, these first seven years represent so to say the blossoming youth of the new-born Christian religion. For princely power had not yet taken over, nor were those other factors present which lend lustre and splendour and confidence but have nothing to do with the true nature of faith. Those years were the happier ones, because the disturbances had not yet broken out that were later caused by the foolhardy peasantry with its wrong-headed counsel, or by the disciplinary measures of the princes, so conducive to war, or by the differences that occurred between the theologians and the Protestant groups.

2. THE RELIGIOUS PERSONALITY

This presentation of the Reformation gives us a portrait of Luther where subjective elements intrude; the intention was not to distort but to stress certain points; not dispensing with accepted ideas, but breathing new life into current orthodox ones.

> I draw Luther out of himself, model him and paint him, and set him up to be seen and admired from the angle which to my mind is the best and most favourable: where he conquers men's minds with arguments drawn from the heavenly treasury of Scripture, and demolishes the manifold cunning attacks of rulers and powers like card castles or painted walls. . . . He may have sinned, may have fallen, in word or deed. . . . That is only so much proof of the weakness of human nature. But doctrine and faith are not thereby affected, for we know what they are based on.

Seckendorf considered the Bible translation Luther's main achievement, he gave it equal rank and importance with the first preaching of Christianity in Germany, a benefit of such immeasurable worth could never be expected to recur. He was utterly convinced that Luther taught the truth, but venerated him less for his doctrine than for his scriptural theology. He did nothing better, he said, his scholarship and his knowledge in this field were unique.

Seckendorf was well versed in Luther's writings. In this respect he had the advantage of contemporary theologians, for usually the latter knew the ' doctrine ' only in the form in which it was approved by the particular school of theology to which they belonged, together with perhaps a portion of the dogmatic literature of the *Konkordienbuch*. There is contemporary evidence for the belief that Luther was hardly read at all in the seventeenth century. According to Seckendorf the situation was even worse than that: not even his dogmatic books escaped the general ignorance. While praising the smaller catechism, he added with a sigh: ' It is to be lamented that this golden little book, very rightly included among the Symbolical Books, is to-day so little read.'

He was not interested in the superhuman and apocalyptical Luther:

> We do not exalt him above other men, and in my book I have never pretended to defend all his words and deeds without distinction. It would have been an injustice to his *manes*, if I may call it so, if I had played the part of a flatterer and not that of a sincere and truthful writer of history.

The important thing was that ' both by persevering defence of doctrine and by steady moral improvement, we may come to be possessed of that same zeal that was so marked in Luther, whether in preaching or in practice.'

3. CHRISTIAN UNIVERSALISM AND REUNION

Seckendorf studied Luther from two points of view: as the author of the Reformation and the Evangelical Church, and as an example of Christian living. Church and piety, dogma and personal belief were conceptions that could still be considered together.

Seckendorf inherited sundry Evangelical traits: for example a disdain of Aristotle and a prejudice against the theologians of the high Middle Ages, a poor opinion of philosophy and uncritical support for the doctrine of justification through faith alone. He gave his whole allegiance to the Lutheran Church with a clear conscience.

> I find nothing to shake the faith in which I was born and brought up and in which I move. That every one must trust his conscience and harken to it—after taking the necessary steps to instruct it—seems to me true without shadow of doubt.
>
> On the other hand, I have not been able to convince myself yet that I should take as binding for eternal salvation the authority and codes of men. It may be attractive to do so, and conducive to a quiet and easy life . . . as long as it is not proved to be prescribed by God as necessary to salvation it can give the spirit no peace.

His confidence in the action of divine providence in history is not specifically Lutheran but eminently Christian. A significant phrase of his—the Reformation as ' the finger of God '—can be misunderstood and taken as an out-and-out affirmation of the Reformation, unless it is brought into line with other remarks. At the Marburg talks on religion in 1529, he said:

> It is true that unity among the two Protestant parties, though so often attempted, was never attained, and that the Lutherans rejected the approaches of their brethren of the Reformed Church. It is also probable that greater progress in the Reformation would have been achieved if the Protestants had been able to unite among themselves. But here too we must pay tribute to the wisdom of divine guidance, which must have had its own motives for permitting this division.

In the same way he traced the breach in the Church caused by the Reformation, a fact he deeply lamented, to men's behaviour and God's providence: for nearly two hundred years it had brought bloodshed and pain to the Christian world, and an incalculable amount of unhappiness, but on the credit side was the clear conscience and the salvation of one of the two protagonists. He, Seckendorf, loved the Reformation, and grieved over it. It was the cardinal point of strife and schism, and had been so from the start up to the time when he wrote. But not only *agente Luthero, sed et hoc dirigente Deo*: it originated in Luther's action, but this too was guided by God.

Un-Lutheran, but far from un-Christian, was a fairer estimation of the Roman Church. The historian, the lover of truth, could not or would not overlook the development that had taken place within Catholicism since the middle of the sixteenth century. He described it as an improvement.

> There are not a few to-day among the Roman clergy whose idea of religion is better than in Luther's day. The one-time neglected study of Holy Scripture has been taken up again. . . . By introducing preaching, instruction, the singing of hymns or such sacred songs as they have adopted in imitation of our purified Church, and also through the removal of certain abuses and the correction of rites, things have gone so far in Germany that in some places, among uneducated people or among those who judge religion by outward appearances, the opinion has grown that our forefathers had no cause, although heavy cause enough was there, to bring that terrible break to pass.

This considerable, if partial, recognition of the Roman Church, and the deep distress of mind in which Seckendorf found himself on account of the breach in the Church, indicate how heavily one thing weighed on his mind: the cause of Christian unity.

Since the beginning of the sixteenth century, in the controversies on dogma unity had been overlooked; through lack of attention it had broken down. And now the pieces would no longer fit together and were a cause of lamentation. In the preface to his work Seckendorf admitted:

What could I more desire than that the light of divine truth might pour into the eyes of all readers and stir their minds, till foes and persecutors became brothers and fellows, acknowledging with us the pure faith with pure hearts and lips, and in common zeal restoring piety of living.

Self-righteousness, a mark of high orthodoxy, was absent in Seckendorf; the desire and longing for Church unity lay at the very core of his thought. There were three questions that specially troubled him: Is it not too late, and utterly in vain, to hope for the unity of the Christian faiths?—What articles of belief are common to the separated faiths, and how far are they fruitful ground for religious communion?—How should the separated faiths and individual Christians of different confessions live together (instead of as foes) in practice?

Fundamentally and in every case, he said, the confessions must put up with one another in all humanity and honesty, it was not only necessary, it was also possible and above all a matter of Christian behaviour; on both sides back-biting and truth-destroying defamation must cease. ' For the things on which we differ are hard enough already. In all (and I speak to the Protestants too) zeal for spreading religion by force, cunning and seducings under a Christian name must be held in check.'

He passionately denied that it was too late and in vain to hope for unity.

To the second question he gave a threefold answer: ' The number and splendour of the articles of faith taught by us all, and the very fact of this must be acknowledged as an act of God's goodness.' Everyone must preach the truth with a pure unfeigned conscience as he himself knows it; and everywhere prayers should be offered up to God that the erring be brought to the truth and those in the truth proceed on their way unswervingly.

To the third question he gave practically the same answer as Francis of Assisi when a Dominican came to him for counsel: he advised him to practise an exemplary Christian way of life. For ' among those kept apart by their views on dogma, there is still easily agreement where piety and virtue are concerned. It is a thing ordinary people know or can easily grasp, when they are not led astray by perverse doctrine.' Moreover he saw no grounds for supposing that common articles of faith could not be defended in common councils against ' unbelievers, atheists and fanatics.'[1]

How far the proposals would be carried out it is not our business to discover. The point is, that after a century and a half of dogmatic differences and recriminations, the time had come when the Christian as such could be seen in the dissenter too, and behind the religious communions separated by their different ' doctrines,' Christianity itself. ' Doctrine ' had been over-stressed. Seckendorf held to it firmly, but no longer identified it with the whole of Christianity. He saw that outside his confession Christianity was also present. The bringing together of all ' Christianities ' in Christian unity was his desire and his intention. The difference was a dogmatic one; ethically there was unity, invisible it is true and without form, but nonetheless there. Lovingly he stressed all that the various Christian parties had in common, preferring *vera pietas* and *virtus*, and instead of dragging into the foreground merely what separated them, as previous generations had done, he gathered together the common heritage and showed that it was considerable. This was his *Christian universalism*.

All this is to be found in a book on Luther and the Reformation. Not accidentally either, but in important places: in the introductory preface and in a retrospective epilogue. The author tells us that these ideas meant a lot to him. He—a Lutheran—had in mind an universal Christian history, free from confessional intolerance. The particular religious impulse which the Reformation brought into Christianity was preferred to the

---

[1] It is undeniable that the idea of Christian unity, having its roots in Christianity itself, can be promoted from outside: by opposition from a non-Christian environment. In practice, defence and attack, directed at a common foe, can serve to sharpen an awareness of what is truly Christian in faith and ethics (as distinct from all that is non-Christian). A threat to the Christian cause as such is more deadly than the threat of inter-confessional strife.

hitherto unassailable Lutheran doctrine. The profoundly religious onset, rather than the dogmatic outcome, was significant.

All this constituted a thoroughgoing reversal of accepted ideas, a quickening reaction to the process of petrification that had set in.

A century and a half had fought for the purity of faith, and Seckendorf had no axe to grind on that score. But in the heat of doctrinal battle care for Christian living had often lapsed. In fact it had come to be looked on with suspicion, as touching justification by works. Here it was that Seckendorf made his stand.

The study of truth and goodness, when they are not put into practice, is not only useless, but positively increases guilt, for those who have more knowledge and insight have the more to account for. It is corruption of morals rather than lack of knowledge that is responsible for the fact that in our day so little of that glowing ardour is seen that our forebears displayed in the early days of the Reformation. Truly nothing more seriously hinders further achievement in our purified religion than relaxation of moral strictness and the open contrast between practical life and holiness of doctrine. That is the reason why many members of other confessions have come to suppose that the breach in the Church was caused by factors which had nothing to do with the urge of conscience and the pure love of truth.

What bound Seckendorf to Lutheran orthodoxy was his faith and churchmanship. But his Christian universalism raised him far above it, and a strong ethical strain was a distinguishing though not a separating factor.

One-sided emphasis on Christian morals and a neglect of dogma amounting to disdain were important features of pietism. And Seckendorf's part in preparing the ground is clear from the high value he set on Christian practice.

In the end the ' human touch ' that Seckendorf so lovingly stressed in Luther became the great theme of the eighteenth century. Except that in the *Aufklärung* its Christian character, still intact in Seckendorf, was lost.[1]

[1] The changes that took place with increasing force within German Protestantism during the last decades of the seventeenth century are only a symptom of the revolution that was taking place in intellectual circles throughout Europe. These seemed to Paul Hazard to be of such importance that he called his brilliant study of the three-and-a-half decades between 1680 and 1715, *La Crise de la Conscience Européenne* (Paris, 1935; English trans., *The European Mind, 1680–1715*, London, 1953).

CHAPTER II
GOTTFRIED WILHELM LEIBNIZ

GOTTFRIED WILHELM LEIBNIZ (1646–1716) was the child of a Lutheran home, attended school and university in Leipzig, travelled, served at princely courts as pundit, and acted in diplomatic missions. Later he was engaged in administration, but administrative duties came second to his interest in land cultivation which absorbed his energies. The last forty years of his life he spent as councillor and librarian in the service of the Duke of Welf (since 1692 Elector) in Hannover. Well known as the founder of differential and integral calculus, and as the philosopher of theodicy,[1] he undertook to prepare from mediæval sources a history of the house of Welf (from the end of the seventh to the beginning of the eleventh century)—a task that covered several decades. He was in fact an all-round genius, of service in all branches, from mining to court law. His activities involved him in constant travel; his sphere was the whole wide world and sometimes he set out for distant cities without waiting for leave of absence.

During the last decade of the seventeenth century, the question of reunion of the churches was a favourite one at the princes' courts. With papal approval, Spinola, the Bishop of Wiener Neustadt (Austria), entered into negotiations with influential men and certain of the princes, the courts of Hannover and Vienna showing most interest. The pope, and the moderate Protestant university of Helmstedt, were not averse to reunion, Louis XIV was opposed to it. Bossuet, since 1670 tutor to the Dauphin, then Bishop of Meaux, in an exchange of letters with Leibniz, took steps to obtain a statement of the dogmatic questions which would have to be settled if reunion were to come about.

Leibniz took part in the discussions held between 1680 and 1700 and also in correspondence with a number of leading men

[1] Theodicy: vindication of divine providence in view of existence of evil (Cf. O.D.).

65

of the reunion movement. There was later some controversy as
to how far what he had written agreed with his personal convic-
tions: was he making a confession of faith, or merely thinking
on paper?

1. THE LUTHERAN REFORMATION

Leibniz was less concerned with Luther the man than with
his cause. But now and again he broke a lance on his behalf:
' It is true that Luther sometimes flared up in an inexcusable way;
but the Lutherans say they are not responsible for his person. . . .'
His line was that Catholics should no more be held responsible
for the faults of bad popes than Protestants for Luther's weaknesses: there is no point in either, except to breed malice.
' Erasmus and a number of excellent men who were not at all
attached to Luther, recognized the necessity of bringing people
back to the teaching of St. Paul. And what they disliked about
Luther was not the deed but the way it was done.'

Leibniz, apparently convinced of the need for the
Reformation, hoped Catholics would equally admit the need,
seeing that ' those views which the Protestants acknowledge as
the best are allowed within the Roman Church itself.' As the
Tridentine Council had condemned basic doctrines of Luther's,
it must have been ideas independent of doctrine as such that
Leibniz imagined to have won the approval of the Roman
Church. Perhaps he was thinking of the decline of scholasticism
and laxity of morals in the Church of 1500, and meant by
Reformation the reform of those evils.

However it may be, he called it a ' time when right views
. . . were smothered under the thorns of countless irrelevancies
which distracted the minds of the faithful and turned them away
from genuine virtue and true theology.' But there was something
else he linked with the Reformation: the rise of science. It is not
impossible that ' true theology ' meant a product of the new
learning. How highly he valued the latter appears in a note he
wrote in 1702:

The darkness of the globe is dispelled by the rise of science and
history, and in the Roman communion men of outstanding

erudition and experience are being discreet rather than ignorant, when they fail to admit how necessary the Reformation was. But it will come, the time when healing truth can let itself be seen everywhere.

Leibniz, though agreeing so far with Catholic dogma, could state that Luther was no heretic.

I cannot see why Luther should rightly be called a heretic; for one cannot mention one single erroneous doctrine that he invented or introduced. He preached against abuses, and that has been recognized as necessary. Sometimes he manifested too much fervour, but on that account no one can be condemned as a teacher of false doctrine.

All goes to show that Leibniz was not prepared to see the Reformation as the overthrow of philosophy. In a chapter of his *Theodicy*, writing on the agreement between faith and reason, he said that when Luther condemned philosophy as the foe of faith, he presumably meant only what he had learnt in the schools, and had not therefore condemned right philosophy at all.

2. LUTHER'S DOCTRINE

Luther and the dogmatic theologians repeatedly insisted that the doctrine of justification by faith alone was the heart and soul of their teaching. Its opposite number, the Catholic doctrine of justification formulated at the Tridentinum, required of a man a contribution of his own, his open assent—the concurrence of his own free will—to the justification offered him by God in Christ. At the sixth session of the general assembly at Trent, in 1547, one year after Luther's death, a number of *canones* were given out as binding in the matter of justification. The first is not far from Luther: ' Whoever holds that man can be justified by God through his works, performed through the powers of his human nature or within the jurisdiction of the Law, without divine grace as present in Jesus Christ, shall be excluded.' The others are mostly directed against Luther. The fourth runs: ' Whoever holds that man's free will does not co-operate when moved and stirred by God in preparing and equipping him for the reception of the grace of justification—be excluded.'

Now in 1680 Leibniz wrote to Prince Ernst von Hessen-Rheinfels, a former Calvinist who had become a Catholic; the prince would, he believed, have come to agree with Philipp Jacob Spener—with whom he had held a theological discussion on justification—if they had gone over the matter point by point. He knew from his own experience that agreement was possible. For in 1670 he, Leibniz, the Protestant, had held long discussion on the same matter with the auxiliary bishop of Mainz,

> and it seemed to us that in practice no difference really existed. I know that in theory (that is in doctrine or dogmatics) one does exist; but in this respect the views of certain Catholics seem to me more reasonable than those of certain Protestants. For love sets a man in a state of grace more than faith does. . . .

In about 1685 he composed a ' *systema theologicum*,' a sort of theory of faith. He examined the nature of justification, and at times his pronouncements are remarkably near to the Tridentine view. He accepted the first Canon, with the ' firm assurance '

> that the nature of man is through the Fall so corrupt that without the help of divine grace it can perform no good work and no deed pleasing to God, nor even make a start alone. Thus, without grace encountering and inciting, no prayer can issue from us, no vow or longing to improve our life or to seek the true faith, and no good impulse at all.

What follows is quite Catholic:

> On the other hand it must be maintained that man's free will was not put in check by the Fall, not even in sacred matters pertaining to salvation; rather, that all acts of the will, whether incited by grace when they are good, or aroused in corrupt nature, when they are bad, yet have the mark of spontaneous choice and are therefore free . . . and although prompting and help come from God, nevertheless co-operation takes place in man, or one could not say he himself took a part in it.

For this reason finally, it is 'to be insisted that justification too, consisting as it does in the remission of punishment, requires not only faith, but repentance and therefore love too.' The 'virtue of love,' Leibniz holds, is poured into us by God because of our inclination to him. But it is of its nature such that it presses us on to activity.

> Therefore (namely because love on the one hand belongs to justification, but on the other hand must act) one can say with certainty that good works, in the form of an earnest will to perform them, are necessary to salvation. For whoever does not love God is not God's friend and does not live in a state of grace, for neither repentance nor regeneration is consequent without love. All good works are, however, virtually (as it is usual to say) contained in a right intention and sincere inclination Godwards, and that is the one thing necessary, of which Christ says it should be preferred to every other.

Writing in 1692 to the French bishop Bossuet, after some testy remarks about Catholic abuses, he declared right doctrine on justification had been reinstated in the Roman Church. On the Lord's Supper dogma he gave cautious assent to the Catholic view in the *systema theologicum* already mentioned:

> Further it is certain that according to the tradition of antiquity a change occurs at the consecration. . . . The new dogma held by certain people, that it is only at the moment of reception that the Body of Christ is present, is in the ancients unheard of.

Both in his personal attitude to the Roman Catholic Church and in the formulation of his ideas on faith, Leibniz differed widely from the Lutheran point of view and Lutheran doctrine. The overtures to Catholicism were undoubtedly there, but are not so relevant as what appears to be a new set of presumptions, never set down in black on white, but simply taken for granted. For example:

> In the last century sharp conflicts broke out on the subject of conversion, and the justification of sinners, and the merit of

good works, one side being tainted by the improper manner of its expression, the other by aggressiveness towards the opponent. I believe it is easily possible to put an end to this sort of thing if they would leave out the sophistries and keep to the matter in hand.

And again:

Whether the power to produce good impulses is destroyed or only hindered in the unregenerate, and what comparisons help to explain grace:—these are matters discussed in a highly unprofitable and artificial manner by those who on all occasions are only on the look-out for mystifications as a means to juggling with Church dogmas with a fair show of righteousness.

Elsewhere he declared that

the question of whether the love of God was necessary to salvation was incomparably more important than the question . . . whether souls have to undergo purification before they attain to the divine vision. Those questions discussed between Rome and Augsburg are merely speculative, whereas the former . . . touches on the very nature of piety.

But only a man quasi indifferent to the authentic teaching of Christ could hold that the great controversies were a mere juggling with sophistries, and that meditation on the state of the soul after death, and its manner of appearing before the face of God, was mere speculation. Leibniz, no enemy of God's word, was however following a different line of thought: ' piety ' was more important than ' doctrine.' Piety was moreover not affected by speculation or dogmatics. ' Practice ' was the same in the different confessions, although ' theory ' was various. Practice and piety, there was the heart of the matter, both being, he held, independent of dogma, so that there was no reason why an institutional union of Christendom should not be effected on the grounds of existing common piety.

Leibniz supported the Reformation, and at the same time he subscribed to a key dogma of Catholicism which was a clear retort to the Reformation. But it is just as incorrect to take his views on the Catholic Church to be secret Catholicism as to read his support of Luther as adherence to Lutheranism.

3. CRITICISM OF THE CHURCHES

The critical independence which characterized Leibniz's attitude to the confessions, applied to his relation to Church and Christianity in general. He was free of confessional prejudice and considered it advisable for the confessions first to correct their own faults and mistakes and only then set about putting each other's houses in order.

He found much to object to in the traditional Evangelical conception of Antichrist, dogmatically a main prop of old Lutheranism. It seemed to Leibniz quite unnecessary to identify the pope with Antichrist. True, he said, many blunders of the Church, and in individual cases the inordinate ambition of churchmen, looked more like anti-Christianity than Christianity. But he added, ' these things in no wise impair the nature of the Church, and as to the assumption that it is actually Antichrist, here I confess my ignorance.' He recommended applying the word Antichrist to whatever was the opposite to Jesus Christ. Spener's aversion to the papal primate, and that of other worthy Protestants, he traced to sheer prejudice: an orthodox explanation of the Apocalypse, strictly within Protestant tradition, had been handed down to them, discovering Rome and the pope in the prophecies of the tower of Babel and Antichrist, and they were unable to shake off the shackles. Catholics were to refrain from dubbing Luther a teacher of heresy, and Protestants to cease to hold the pope to be Antichrist. He stated categorically: ' If the pope were to take his stand on reason and the Protestants still insisted he was Antichrist, they would be proper schismatics.'

He was not uncritical of the Roman Church, but more critical of its past than of its actual state. His idea of Church history had something of the clear rationality of Melanchthon. He cut down the period of ecclesiastical darkness to two hundred and fifty years, from 1250 to 1500, and produced arguments from history, not from the *Apocalypse*, to explain this

' darkness.' Not Satan but the ' artifices of the clerics caused Germany to be without a lord and master ' at that time. And with the decay of the state, justice, peace and learning went by the board too. In theology, ' sophistry took the place of clear instruction.' Moreover ' in the tenth century the darkness that descended upon the Church by degrees never reached such a pitch,' for right theology, proper instruction on the sacraments, and the Christian way of life of the clergy were the rule in Germany. This state of affairs broke down only when ' the Roman bishops thrust themselves forward as lords of the Church and their emissaries the mendicant friars took possession of the schools.'

After the failure of the plans for reunion, he wrote:

I, who cannot allow that purity of worship be repressed through direct or indirect action of Rome, nor that, in spite of the separation from the East, Christianity be made the object of men's disgust and ridicule, and through the barbarity of the times, an unreasonable theology unknown to Christ's apostles appear in the world—I have nonetheless steadily desired that the authority of the first bishop's see and the old form of the hierarchy be reinstated, on the condition laid down by Melanchthon when he signed the Schmalkaldic Article: Only if the popes make room for the Gospel of Christ.

In January 1684 he wrote to Landgrave Ernst:

I say that the [Catholic] hierarchy as seen there [in Rome] with the exaltation of the first bishop is properly and divinely right, for bishops and priests must have a superior. I will further add that the visible Catholic Church is, thanks to the special subvention of the Holy Spirit as promised, infallible on all articles of faith necessary to salvation.

Ten years later, however, in a hasty reply to Mme de Brinon, the French friend of the Princess, who wished to enter into conversation with him, he wrote: ' I have admitted the advantages of your party but I have also recognized that they are cancelled out by reliable and much stronger reasons.' He did not go into the question of advantages and disadvantages, but in 1692 he gave Bossuet an indication of what he meant:

> To-day when right doctrine on justification has been restored in the Roman Church, as ill luck would have it other abuses have grown up, and the people are led astray from that prayer in spirit and in truth which is the very essence of religion, and turn to confraternities and other such fashions which do not make much headway in Rome itself but are all too effective elsewhere.

We may well wonder what to make of all this: criticism of the Roman form of worship ' and other abuses,' together with the highest appraisal of Roman doctrine, institutions and authority. Recognition of the Reformation and its author as historical facts, hand in hand with the rejection of Lutheran dogma, but always with the amending clause that Luther was no heretic. The core of the matter was prayer in spirit and in truth, and Leibniz volunteered no further elucidation either on one side or the other.

What is really astonishing is that such an attitude was possible to a thoughtful systematic mind such as Leibniz the genius possessed. From the dogmatic point of view, whether Catholic or Lutheran, his remarks appear incredibly incoherent. We will however see as we go along how they can be inter-related from another standpoint.

4. REUNION

Leibniz took a much milder view of the opposition between Christian faiths than earlier generations had done. If like Seckendorf he underlined points in common rather than divergencies, he laid such stress on the similarities that the divergencies were submerged. The differences between the Lutherans and the Reformed Church (Calvinistic) were mere speculations; the differences in forms of worship as between Catholics and Protestants were more important than dogmatic differences. The latter he minimized, making light of them. With an adjustment in practice of religious observances, he considered reunion was a possibility:

I am therefore of the opinion that if Rome would only alter its practice and discipline . . . and tone down its dogmatic condemnations, the schism could be closed and in such a manner that I believe fundamentally the dogma of the Tridentine Council and the *Confessio* of Pius IV could remain, although the *punctum facti*, whether the Tridentine Council was œcumenical and whether certain dogmas are necessary, be left open.

Of course Leibniz was right, that religious discussions and a council were the only means of being rid of schism without bloodshed and of restoring unity without war. He could not see why schism should exist at all. If only the ' parties ' (as he began to call them) would set to work everywhere on the basis of reason, agreement was bound to be reached. His active support of reunion was not only due to his concern as a Christian for the indivisibility of the mystical body of Christ in its visible form, more important here are his endeavours on philosophical grounds to restore all things to unity and uniformity.[1]

He sketched his views in a letter to Mme de Brinon:

First, certain points of Protestant doctrine must be respected, such as communion in both species, marriage of the clergy, use of the vernacular, etc. Secondly, the articles of faith and those of controversy should be set out in some such manner as M. de Meaux' [Bossuet's], so that at least in the eye of a number of adaptable moderate Protestants, it would be clear that if taken in such and such a sense, such doctrines are, if not actually all wholly true, at least not wholly damnable from a Protestant viewpoint. Thirdly, certain offences and abuses in practice should be done away with: they might annoy the Protestants, and the Church itself and pious cultured

---

[1] Leibniz' conception of Church unity corresponded to his subtle ideas on unity of Empire (cf. Erik Wolf, ' Idee und Wirklichkeit des Reiches im deutschen Rechtsdenken des 16. und 17. Jahrhunderts,' in Larenz, *Reich und Recht in der Philosophie*; I 33, sq., especially pp. 159 sqq.) and may possibly be traced to the fundamental idea of *ordo*.

people regard them with disapproval; it should then be possible for each to communicate according to the rites of the other, and the ecclesiastical hierarchy could be restored. Differences of opinion on remaining articles are no more an obstacle to this [the restoration of the hierarchy, etc.] than [a number of controversial points within the Roman Church itself, which are at least as important as those affected by the Augsburg–Rome controversy] . . . It must be a foregone conclusion that any decision the Church may one day reach in a new œcumenical council be taken as binding. Such a council would have to be above reproach in form, and attendance at it should be open to the Protestant nations through their prelates and general superintendents, who would be accepted as bishops, recognized by His Holiness, in just the same way as the bishops of Catholic nations.

Unity was corporate unity, as understood at that time. The Catholics need only to close an eye to a few major claims of the Protestants, in compensation the Protestants could let pass a few articles of Catholic faith, but they would have to be put in a form acceptable to the sons of the Reformation. Hierarchical reunion was to be built on a foundation of mutual friendly tolerance.

Politically, or diplomatically, considered, reunion should be the outcome of negotiations and concessions, as customary between the cabinets of the European kingdoms. Reference to a council was a wise suggestion, the need for its decisions to be binding was even wholly Catholic, but all in all it was too shallow, too unstable, a basis for the mending of broken Christendom.

We are struck at how far Leibniz had moved away from Luther. Protestant ' doctrine ' had so profoundly changed that he took it to be much the same as Catholic doctrine. He accorded infallibility to a council that was in Luther's view guilty of error, and the papacy that Luther declared to be the seat of the Antichrist he would have established, together with the hierarchy, supreme over the Protestant churches.

Nonetheless Leibniz was never a Catholic, either secretly or publicly.

5. THE CONFESSIONAL CHURCHES

At the age of thirty-eight Leibniz made an admission to Landgrave Ernst:

After all these explanations, your Illustrious Highness will ask: Why don't you go over? The answer: Even if the Church is infallible in matters of faith pertaining to salvation, it may happen that inside the Church itself certain errors and bad habits of another kind creep into men's minds, and if acquiescence is demanded, it is impossible to remain in communion if one is honest. For instance, when the Jansenists were required to sign a certain statement about a certain fact, believing the opposite to be true, it was not within their power to obey, even at the risk of being turned out of the communion of the faithful. This not only occurs in regard to facts that appear true to the mind, but also to questions that depend on the exercise of reason. For instance, suppose the Holy Father considered the spherical form of the earth an absurdity, actually opposed to the analogy of faith, and demanded a disavowal from the astronomers of the day; or supposing the Church of to-day demanded of astronomers a disavowal of the Copernican system! It is quite clear there would have been a number of distinguished astronomers who would have found it impossible to assent without hypocrisy: scientific opinions are not dependent on volition, to be altered at choice. To return to my own case, I hold certain philosophic views to be proved, at the present stage of my intellectual formation I cannot alter them as long as I do not see how to refute the grounds on which I hold them. Now it happens that these views are disapproved of by the school theologians who are persuaded that the contrary is *de fide*; they are even censured from time to time, although to my knowledge they contradict neither Holy Scripture nor tradition nor the definitions of any council whatever. It might be suggested I should keep these scruples to myself in order to avoid censure, but that will not do. For the opinions concerned are of great philosophic weight, and if I were to make a statement one day about the considerable discoveries I believe myself to have made, in matters concerning the examination of truth and the advancement of human learning, I must be able to present them as fundamental. Actually, if I had been born in the Roman Church, I would not leave it until I was turned out, but as I was born and brought up outside the Roman communion, I believe it to be dishonest and very unsafe to seek for admission when one knows one would not be accepted if one laid one's heart bare. Moreover one would constantly be under pressure to conceal one's views or to expose oneself to a *turpius ejicitur quam non admittitur hospes* [it is worse for the newcomer to be ejected than never to be admitted]. It would give scandal to a great many people and for me it would mean not peace but very great confusion of mind; quite apart from the danger to one's very existence as a citizen if one lapsed. Anyhow these opinions may be damned by the monks, they are permitted or at least tolerated by profoundly pious and profoundly enlightened bishops and theologians; but it is too uncertain a matter to expose oneself on the strength of a *perhaps*, and one would have to try and be clear about it beforehand. I have often and for many years thought it over, but I have not yet found a way out. . . . Could your Illustrious Highness help to rid me of my perplexity? I readily admit I had rather be in the Roman communion at any cost, if I could only go with true peace of mind and a quiet conscience such as I now enjoy; for I know well enough that I for my part leave no stone unturned to attain to such desirable union and its attendant joys. . . .

When nearing fifty, he answered the same question with considerably more resignation. He admitted that ever since he was twenty-two his mind had been occupied with the question of going over to the Roman Church, and he had been urged to do so by such famous men as Walenburch, the auxiliary bishop, Boineburg, the prime minister of the Elector of Mainz, and the Hannoverian duke Johann Friedrich—all of them converts.

If social advantage or ambition had been my idols, measure for yourself[1] whether a young man could withstand such powerful inducements, to which my conscience stood alone in solitary opposition. I admit the merits of your party, but I recognize too that they are cancelled out by reliable and much stronger reasons . . . of philosophical concern. To rid oneself of them would be as though someone said, Rid yourself of the truth: for philosophy means simply this. It might be that a sectarian philosophy was meant, but I am a long way from being able to philosophize along those lines. One is actually within a sect when one lays too much stress on human authority and the interests of one party.

In appearing to stand above both confessions, Leibniz actually stood outside both. He had outgrown strict Lutheranism, could make little of its doctrine, and saw beyond its bounds a living theology and a pious Christian way of life which struck him as being not at all damnable in the lump. His Catholic leanings showed a complete absence of the principles on which a man like Johann Gerhard built the dogmatic structure of Lutheran Christianity. But he held Catholicism at arm's length too, the bar being that he might lose his freedom for philosophical research. Between the two he enjoyed a peace of mind he feared to lose, and the conscience that stood in his way was not a Protestant but a philosophic one. Not that the truths philosophy had opened up were opposed to Roman dogma, in fact his reasons for not becoming a Catholic appear fidgety rather than effectual: the theologians were responsible for the obstacles, he considered, and he did not want to get into difficulties with them.

If the matter in hand had been the eternal salvation of the immortal soul, these were no valid grounds for refusal—but that was far from Leibniz' mind. As he took pains to explain, one could be in inner communion with the Catholic Church. Moreover, a confessional communion was after all only a party with human authority and with advantages and disadvantages about equally balanced—a view he favoured especially in later years.

[1] To Mme de Brinon.

He picked and chose from the different confessions what pleased him most, and fitted the pieces together. It was a sort of Christian universalism; but the way he did it was liberal and rational.

Long and often have I invoked God's aid and set the party spirit aside as far as a man is capable of it; as though I were new-born, no party member yet, coming from another world, I studied the controversies; I finally decided on my own account for this and that, with due weighing of all relevant circumstances, as Holy Scripture, pious antiquity, right reason itself and sound historical studies require of an impartial man.

One may state that the parties have three principles: (1) The authority of tradition; (2) Scripture; (3) Philosophy. Authority guides the Roman and Greek Churches principally; Scripture the Protestants; Philosophy the Socinians [modern: Unitarian]. All three principles are good. But they can be abused, and that gives rise to errors.

The high status accorded to learning, science, affected his whole way of life too. A mature Protestant seen as 'a man without pre-conceived notions' had a certain field of faith and knowledge available in which he sought independently for matter appealing to his reason as suitable to guide him through life. It came to this: man no longer wanting to consider himself open to criticism from dogma—or to put it more precisely, from God, but judging from dogma for himself, or to put it more precisely, now he would judge God. Reason, in Leibniz' view, although extremely independent, was yet Christian and not opposed to belief. But the lines along which independent reason was to run when belief grew pallid or died, appeared in the course of eighteenth-century *Aufklärung* history, as Lessing and Frederick the Great were to show.

Leibniz, still embedded in the Christian faith and tradition, nonetheless gives clear evidence of the change that overcame men's minds in Germany round the year 1700, leading to the separation of pietism and rationalism from orthodox Christianity, or in other words, to the separation of piety of a critical, ethical kind from belief based on dogma. Leibniz' part in working out a

new idea of the Reformation and a corresponding conception of
Luther was decisive, whether conscious or not. He was responsible
for the decline of exclusive confessionalism. The unity of the
Church was more important to him than the ' doctrines ' of the
confessions with their strong dogmatic trend. The confession as
such ceased to be important, Church and Christianity remained.
He was not only a peace-maker, but a witness for the Irenian
tendency that spread in Germany and Europe after the bloodshed
of religious strife. Moreover the dissolution of dogma set in with
Leibniz, who took it as a means of comparison rather than the
transcription of mystical reality; and ' the real thing ' he was
inclined to see in the practice of devotion.

Lutheran was his attitude to conscience, except that his
conscience urged him to quite a different set of activities from
Luther's. Lutheran influence showed in his positive estimate of
the Reformation and its author. But un-Lutheran was his attitude
to doctrine. The importance he attached to religious morality
connected him with pietism, and reason with rationalism; with
Catholicism his preference for hierarchy, Church unity and a
general council. All through went a strain of universalism in
which the idea of the *una sancta ecclesia catholica* also ran but not
dominant.

Let there be no mistake about it: the dream was of a structure
of world-wide, all-embracing secular universalism, founded not
on Christian belief but on natural thought-processes.

Thus in Leibniz we see a turning point: the two principles of
the Reformation being freedom of conscience, conducing to
faith, and the justification doctrine, concerning the content of
faith; for the first time in history the former rose victorious
over the latter.

CHAPTER III

PIETISM

1. PHILIPP JACOB SPENER

PIETISM began with Philipp Jacob Spener (1635–1705). It is called after the gatherings held under Spener's direction: the *collegia pietatis*. Spener was an Alsatian by birth, from Rappoltsweiler. He was a theological student in Strasbourg under Johann Conrad Dannhauer[1] and later preacher for a few years in the same city. From 1666 to 1686 he was in charge of a parish in Frankfurt am Main, then principal preacher to the court of Dresden, and in 1691 provost of the Nikolaikirche in Berlin, where he remained until his death. During the last ten years of his life the new Prussian university of Halle, where Christian Thomasius and August Hermann Francke taught, became under his influence a stronghold of pietism. The controversy between strict Lutherans and pietists began in his lifetime, a controversy —as both parties understood it—as to the nature of Christianity and the form of church and inward disposition proper to it. Both parties were Evangelical, both appealed to Luther. It was a thorough-going contest as to the ' genuine ' Luther—fought not on Luther's account but for the Christian cause. Two quite different views were in question, but Martin Luther's authority was still so compelling that neither of the controversialists cared to dispense with him as king's evidence for their respective position.

(a) TRADITIONAL IDEAS

There were various degrees of pietism, some more moderate some more radical. Spener was far from radical. What he desired was that religion should be deeply and personally inward and faith be made effective in active works, but all within the strict framework of the Lutheran Church itself—inevitably he

[1] Cf. Part I, Ch. III.

81

considered. As Leibniz observed, he stood foursquare on firm Lutheran ground.

Among a number of passages showing his traditional allegiance is one on Luther's 'service' in making Antichrist better known than ever before and in disposing of him to some extent. He too saw Antichrist in the pope, and found cause for loud lamentation when a wave of Catholicism spread over East Prussia on the conversion of Johann Philipp Pfeiffer, professor of theology in Königsberg (1694). It affected 'numbers of distinguished families' and 'large numbers of students,' and inspired his urgent prayer: 'May God himself restrain the spread of the papacy, here publicly, there secretly—to the growth of which we ourselves have too much contributed, to the provocation of divine justice.'

Of Luther, he wrote in exactly the same spirit as the strict Lutherans of the seventeenth century, that since apostolic times ' there was hardly one who had seen in a clearer light the doctrine of the saving power of faith,' or expounded it better than the reformer. He cultivated his memory by reading him: 'But I affirm I have not only diligently read him, I love him from the bottom of my soul.' He had an affinity for Luther's type of religion, took him as his model and on one occasion called him ' my worthiest predecessor.' His admiration for Luther's reformation and all his achievements in this field was so great, he could not mention it without thanking God for the 'instrument by means of which he accomplished the blessed work of the Reformation.'

I say so again, Luther was a beloved man of God, a gift for whom we cannot be too thankful to God, as much on account of the blessed work of the Reformation, the contest with the papacy, and many useful books, as on account of the incomparable German translation of Holy Scripture. . . . In what concerns Luther, I never deny that I not only hold his memory sacred, but could not do otherwise but on all occasions extol the grace which the All-Highest granted him, and through him the Church.

(b) NEW EVALUATIONS

(i) Luther

In the orthodox seventeenth century this high estimation of Luther was in vogue. But in Spener we find assumptions which are completely absent in strict Lutheranism.

He took exception to quite a number of current forms of adulation: ' I must admit I do not understand our excessive adulation of Luther, practically making an idol of him . . .' He preached reverence and an ' imitation of Luther ' of a very different kind from that of the orthodox Lutherans, indeed in flat contradiction to it. ' If this same Luther were to rise up to-day he would not recognize his followers as disciples, for they often apply themselves quietly to reinstate in the Church certain principles which he most heartily contested with the papists.' The orthodox Lutherans were much more clear-sighted in their adherence to the justification theory than Spener and his company. He could not and would not accuse them of deviation from their creed, but did accuse them of using papistical methods to maintain it pure. This he saw as a restraint on conscience, but saw it as a papistical, not an Evangelical restraint.

The move away from dogmatic Christianity over to unrestrained individual piety was now well launched, and Spener's was a test-case, showing the change at every stage.

Luther was not so much the perpetrator of the faith as the most faithful witness of Evangelical truth: Spener went back to the source of Luther's inspiration, the Bible itself. He recognized no court of reference for safeguarding the manner and method of Bible interpretation, considering the idea on principle papistical.

The Bible was authority, but not Luther. Spener was free to criticize him and on occasion did so, displeased at his vehemence. He considered that ' humanly ' he was not always praiseworthy: like the Calvinists in Berlin against whom Paul Gerhardt had stormed,[1] he was for distinguishing between Luther's gifts and Luther's weaknesses, and moreover he felt it incumbent on him

[1] Cf. Part I, Ch. III, p. 50.

to point out with some emphasis the difference between Luther's version and the canonical version of the Bible.

> Highly as I esteem Luther, I do recognize he is but man and set him far far below the apostles . . . not to speak of his exposition of Scripture, and particularly of the prophets, where the beloved man was insufficiently equipped and often missed the meaning . . . and in other passages where a number of natural traits have crept in . . . and various passages have been so pulled about, it can clearly be shown that was not the original meaning of the text. . . .

The very suggestion that the Bible translation could be improved was offensive to strict Lutheranism, and especially the idea that Luther had not always rightly construed the text, for the doctrine of justification, the very foundation stone of Lutheranism, was itself simply a Lutheran reading of Scripture. Besides, if a man stood up and said Luther was sometimes wrong, he might personally draw the line at the doctrine of justification and the related doctrines of original sin and lack of free will— he laid the way open to criticism independent of Luther.

Spener undoubtedly accepted Luther's personal human authority, while rejecting his dogmatic authority on the grounds that it is ' a necessary piece of Christian freedom . . . to be no man's slave.'

Chiefly to be valued in Luther, and of great importance, was the bringing of freedom from man-made codes and intellectual violence—not the fact that Luther founded the doctrine of justification, but more generally, that he concentrated on the Bible, was what constituted the greatness of the Reformation for Spener.

(ii) Faith

At a first glance it may appear that Spener was a true follower of the reformers in his teaching on faith. He was out and out convinced that ' the law ' could produce neither good works nor conversion to God; man could be justified only through faith, ' that is purely by the grace of God with no adulteration of works.' But just as important as the command to believe was the putting of it into effect. He demanded ' tokens of true faith ' in the name of Luther. He distinguished between ' pure doctrine ' and ' pure faith,' which he held to be bound up with a certain form of piety.

Very surprising to strict Lutheran ears was this new call to piety. Spener called it ' pure faith '; but its activating function turned it into ' works,' in fact ' good works ' in a much more massive sense than the much-decried ' works ' of the Catholic doctrine of justification, requiring simply that a man shall of his own free will open himself to the reception of divine grace. . . .

By saving faith, Spener and the pietists meant an inner power and an inner light urging a man to the religious life. It was expressed in prayer, love of neighbour, love of God. It was more important than the letter of ' doctrine ' and was conducive to salvation: and this light lit in a man was termed ' saving.' Significantly, the light of faith was independent of confession and doctrine, other Christians could share it. From now on, exclusive confessionalism was doomed. As Spener put it: he hesitated to say, ' *Lutheranus qua Lutheranus salvatur*, which would mean all Lutherans were saved. But whoever was to be saved (from this or that communion) must be saved *qua fidelis*, namely *fide salvifica*.'

(iii) *Conscience*

With this conception of faith went a corresponding one of conscience, for Spener ' our main principle of our whole religion.' He meant by it the freedom of personal conviction. Whoever touched conscience was offending against the very nature of Evangelical Christianity—a thesis which put orthodoxy out of the saddle. For the Lutheran regional churches with their princes as senior bishops and their consistories were declared to be, as far as organization was concerned, so many small papacies. When these authorities, he argued, made decisions (as indeed they did), saying this is to be believed, that to be shunned, and those decisions had binding power on the people living within their political sphere of influence, then it was a papistical principle, and thus

the Lutheran regional churches gave tacit assent to the papists.
' If it is a matter of human authority, then their band (the papists')
is the greatest and most considerable and has in many respects
the advantage of us. . . . With us it not only can happen,
but actually does happen, that whole collegia and faculties
speak contrary to one another, which with them does not
happen. . . .' For him the very nerve of Christianity was, as he
put it, to ' thank God in eternity that he let us recognize in truth
that we must not trust in the authority of one or many men but
in our Saviour Jesu Christo, who is Himself the truth and reveals
Himself in His word and through the same in the hearts of His
own who seek Him; and that they in no wise submit their
conscience to other men. . . .' That was in a statement made
in 1678. Ten years later he elaborated his point in a letter:
' Hence my liberty remains, without bonds and depending on
no man as such, and I need accept nothing from any man except
in so far as he can convince me from the clear word of God, so
that conscience may be at rest. As I so often remind my hearers:
not to believe the least thing from me without proving it in
God's word.'

Luther claimed the right to let himself be lit by the word of
God, and Spener made the same claim for every Christian.
With far more warmth than Leibniz, he seized upon the principle
of freedom of conscience independent of all human authority,
and raised it to be the very *raison d'être* of the Reformation and
Christianity.

So now Reformation stood over against Reformation, Luther
over against Luther. The two different principles—the doctrine
of justification, and freedom of conscience—though combined
in Luther himself at the well-head of the Reformation, were now
on opposite sides, antagonists.

(iv) *Reformation*

Spener never despised ' pure doctrine,' only it was less than
piety and freedom of conviction. People committed to the
justification doctrine were bound to envisage the Reformation

as dogmatically rounded off and not subject to further development. What interested Spener was the dynamic of the Reformation, and he saw it as something at the same time more powerful and less compatible with ' doctrine ' than Seckendorf, his senior by ten years.

It was no bygone event, but remained unfinished, a task still to be pursued. He thanked God for the benefits accrued to the Church through Luther's work, but admitted ' readily that it stopped too soon.' He compared it to the return from Babylon which did actually occur, but for the building of Jerusalem and the Temple only the ground was ready, neither was built as yet, whereas much evil of Babylonian origin had slipped in too. He was not prepared to consider the state of the Church in Luther's lifetime as ideal, even after it had been reformed, and what was still to be desired and still to be done must be taken in hand.

The setting up of the regional church system seemed to him to miss the mark completely. It struck him as sheer oppression to put the Church under secular authority. It weighed on his conscience, as a contradiction of Christianity and the spiritual nature of the Church. But it was the Reformation seen as the improvement of morals and devotion that was so unfinished.

In the early sixteenth century, he said, people knew nothing at all about the justification doctrine but were fairly at home with the doctrine of good works. That is why Luther's preaching always heavily stressed the need for faith, so much so that it seemed as though ' he extolled that alone and positively rejected works,' but that was never what he meant. The opposite situation had now arisen in the outgoing years of the seventeenth century, and more attention to God's salvation was required, because one had to deal with people who knew about the doctrine of the gospel, but nothing at all of the duty of Christian good works.

We must with great earnestness contest the error [that good works are unnecessary], no less dangerous than that other [that a man is justified by good works] and extol above all the power by which faith becomes active, through love and holy living; though we must not forget the need to remember that what saves us is not holy living but faith itself. Just as our Luther in his day emphasized the one but never lost sight of the other. Divine doctrine is always one and the same, only at certain times and for certain people one part of it has to be more earnestly inculcated than at other times and for other people.

Here in the spiritual sphere was an early version of the idea of improvement which, after secularization, was, as ' progress,' to rule men's minds throughout the eighteenth and nineteenth centuries and right into the twentieth.

(v) *Tolerance and Church*

Spener's conception of faith and conscience placed him in a new relation to the other confessions, a wide departure from the intolerance of orthodox Lutheran practice.

Theologically, intolerance had its roots in the fact that confessional doctrine was held to be the only right interpretation of Christianity and membership of the confession an essential condition for attaining to salvation. Each of the three great confessions—Catholic, Lutheran, Calvinist—held the others to have been led into error by Satan.

Spener in the main admitted the connexion between confessional church and salvation, but he shook it loose. He thanked God for entrusting his word to the Evangelical Church and maintaining it there. He called this the Church's ' great advantage over all false sects and religions,' and believed he could on this account ' acknowledge it with good right as alone the visible Church of Christ.'

The means to salvation he called Church and faith, explaining both in his own way. He took as his starting-point the ' common catchword ': ' *extra ecclesiam nulla salus*.' This, he said, ' undoubtedly refers to the invisible Church and the spiritual communion which true believers have with their head Jesu Christo and among one another as members.' The invisible Church was the real one.

It was not based on confession or ' particular church,' but on baptism as a prerequisite, to which must be added, in individual men, faith in the form of a light lit in the heart by God—' the only means to our salvation, uniting us to God.' That outside the Evangelical Church there was no salvation, he only admitted with the sharp distinction that by 'Evangelical Church' should be understood no visible and actual institutional Church, but ' the inward communion of faith.'

It was quite conceivable for a man to possess, ' according to the measure granted him,' a lively faith in Christ as the source of salvation, 'even though he cannot know of our (Evangelical) communities, where they may be and how they are distinct from others in their visible constitution.' Such a man is latently Evangelical, independently of what communion he belongs to.

A wedge had now been driven between the public confession of faith and the inner light of faith. Not the Church but the individual conscience was responsible for the salvation of the soul. Conscience in Spener became so all-important that it resented as pressure and oppression contact with any authority whatever, apart from the Bible.

Individualism and subjectivism were the marks of a new form of Christianity, seen now through pietist eyes as the relation of the individual to God. The attitude of the individual became the criterion of what was Christian. The objective standards preserved in dogma yielded to subjective *intention*. The principle of freedom was invoked, not for the Church and not for the communion, but for the individual. The supernatural authority of communion and Church was thus made dubious. Whether he knew it or not, Spener had sown the seed of revolution.

A consequence of Spener's principle of individual freedom was freedom in expounding the Bible, which meant freedom to form one's own theological opinions; at a further remove, other consequences were to be the non-binding nature of accepted Church dogma; freedom of decision according to conscience, whether the word of the Bible is to be taken for truth or not; freedom to believe or not to believe; freedom to be a Christian or not.

2. GOTTFRIED ARNOLD

During the last decades of the seventeenth century, Gottfried Arnold planned and completed his comprehensive and so-called ' non-party ' *History of Church and Heresy*. He was a mystical writer and a composer of hymns. The History appeared in 1699 in Frankfurt. The author was born in 1666 in the Erzgebirge, studied theology, knew Spener in Dresden, and was for a short time professor of Church history at the university of Giessen. After a period of radical religious enthusiasm, which caused him to break with the Church and reject marriage as a Christian institution, he returned to his former ordered way of life, married in 1701 and took on parish work. His last parish was at Perleberg on the Elbe, where he died in 1714 aged eighty-four.

He was forty years younger than Seckendorf, thirty years younger than Spener and twenty years younger than Leibniz. His Church History appeared at the very time when Seckendorf's *Historia Lutheranismi* (1692) was becoming popular and when Spener and Leibniz had both matured. What he owed to these men is strongly apparent. It is not clear (and it does not matter) how far he was aware of it. One is constantly coming across themes which had occupied his elders, but his own contribution was more considerable than his debt to these others. Mention of Luther occurs fairly frequently, and he also published a *Lives of the Faithful* which contains a biography of the reformer, exclusively confined to his personal piety: ' The life of Dr. Martin Luther, of a purpose founded on his inner motions.' But the second part of the History gives us the more relevant information.

(a) LUTHER'S BEGINNINGS PREFERRED

It was Seckendorf who had started the fashion of preferring a young, impulsive Luther to the old reformer and church-founder bent on giving his work a dogmatic base.

Spener showed up the difference between Luther young and Luther old, and Arnold played one off against the other.

All that was left of the old orthodox type of veneration for Luther was the high praise for his natural gifts, hearty ways and heroic courage. The Reformation was still an act of God and Luther still God's instrument, but it was all put in a way that the *Aufklärung* itself was to find quite satisfactory: the first thirty years of Luther's life, guided by Divine Providence, were wholly devoted to the Reformation. All he learnt, all he experienced, was from God, the better to prepare him to see the necessity for a reformation. This included the founding of Wittenberg university, Luther's advancement as a monk through his Superior Staupitz, his appreciation of the Pauline epistles, his visitations of monasteries, and much else.

At the beginning of his Wittenberg activities, Martin Luther was 'the perfect model of a true Evangelical Christian and teacher, verily mightily guided and used by God as a beloved instrument of his grace.'

If we question the strict Lutherans of the seventeenth century as to what special graces Luther received, we shall be given the unanimous answer: the grace of acknowledging true Evangelical doctrine, meaning the doctrine of justification of the sinner without merit of his own, through faith alone. Gottfried Arnold's answer is: Clearly God gave him as a gift ' the acknowledgement of his true gospel, or his will to redeem men through faith.'

Apparently the same answer twice over. But Arnold meant something quite different. He still made use of the old Protestant differentiation of law and gospel, human merit and Christ's merit. But for Luther and the orthodox the ' evangelium ' was contained in the Pauline passage on justification,[1] for Arnold it had no point when not preceded by ' the revelation of Jesus Christ in the heart.' Mystical revelation was granted to Luther in his years in the monastery. It is of supreme importance, and dogmatic allegiance, being dependent on it, carries less weight.

Luther in his youth hurled himself upon ' true salvation,' ' only to be obtained through grace and union with Jesus Christ.' Arnold stressed his honest behaviour (he called Erasmus to witness[2]) and valued the persecutions and temptations to which

---

[1] *Romans* i, 17; iii, 24.

[2] Leibniz called Erasmus to witness for the opposite contention: what Erasmus disliked in Luther was not the deed but the manner of it.

Luther was exposed because they kept him constant in watching and praying: 'These righteous exercises and struggles kept his heart in humility at that time and nicely subdued that original pride rooted in all men.'

For Arnold, Luther's reformation consisted in making Christ the middle point of the life of faith, after his own personal experience of spiritual union with Christ. Hence his divine appointment to carry out the Reformation, upon which Johann Gerhard had so strongly insisted,[1] was now of far less importance than his immediate vocation through the spirit by means of the inner light. Indeed he rated the unrecorded inspiration of Luther so highly that it was second to nothing, not even the written word of the Bible.

(b) LUTHER'S PERSONALITY CRITICIZED

Considering Luther as man and individual, Arnold approved of the degree of piety and morality observable in him; in common with the orthodox, he valued his ' natural ' gifts, courage and presence of mind; but severely criticized certain idiosyncrasies: his vehemence, his passionate ways, the indecency and immodesty of many of his utterances, his aggressiveness, his licentiousness in speech, writing and behaviour—all these were crimes and no small ones.

Moreover Luther's followers followed him chiefly in licentiousness of living. For when the old Adam in the Lutherans inclined to indulge in worldly affections, it was very convenient to fall back on the sacrosanct person of the founder.

When for example it is known far and wide and even told from the pulpit, how on Shrove Tuesday Luther let some mumming mimers in and . . . played with them . . . singing and leaping about. . . . What is commended here but corrupt nature itself, which as even the children's catechism points out, is to die in the old Adam. He who daily sees and bemoans the wickedness of the people in drink will find it unnecessary to have such things held up for admiration. So many people

[1] Cf. Part I, Ch. III, pp. 39-44.

disapprove of dear Luther for recommending outward pleasures as a cure for melancholy, for example ' riding, hunting, making merry in good company,' especially as he added: ' as long as it be done in the fear of God, to his furtherance and honour, a word or a jest more or less is neither here nor there: God were well pleased.' Whether this does not concern the mortifying of the flesh rather than its sphere and freedom; that is to say, whether it is, on the example of the men taught and sent by God (*Isaias* x, 2, 3; *Ezechiel* iv, 12, 15), to be excused (as does happen) is easily determined.

Though Gottfried Arnold did find really bad examples of Luther's coarse manner of address, taken all in all his approach was conducive to a dangerously narrow outlook. To over-emphasize the moral side of piety was to present Christian perfectibility in a wrong light. It was this narrow point of view that produced a type of worthy, but physically and spiritually strait-laced people, who in the eighteenth and still more in the nineteenth century were a dead-weight on Christianity, because their type of piety came to be the sole criterion for determining whether a man was worth anything or not—as in the case of Nietzsche.

Gottfried Arnold inclined to see the overcoming of the old Adam as moral achievement rather than sacramental, invisible reality. From now on subjectivism was rife in Evangelical Christianity. God's action in men through the sacraments was not denied, but stress was laid chiefly on prayer, deeds, conduct.

(c) THE IDOLIZING OF LUTHER CRITICIZED

The uncritical reverence and awe of the orthodox attitude to Luther was due to seeing him as bearer and propounder of the only truth making for salvation. Gottfried Arnold took a different line. Dealing out criticism with a free hand for the sake of conscience and truth, he was determined to find out what hindered the spread of the ' evangelium.' He blamed disunity among Lutherans and the fact that Luther himself deviated in certain respects from his original lines. This accusation he set down as follows: ' Before the eyes of God, to whom we must give account as far as in us lies for all our words, and in no way purporting to blacken this excellent instrument . . . (only not through unfounded praise) to falsify the story.' For the right in conscience to dare to criticize Luther he fell back on a word of Melanchthon's pupil Joachim Camerarius: ' Whoever considers it blameworthy to say anything derogatory about the deficiencies of great and famous people has far too mild an idea of these people's condition. For God alone has the advantage of being without fault; human nature is not capable of this.'

He felt he could well dispense with the superlatives the orthodox showered upon their Church founder. Strictly speaking, Luther was neither an apostle nor a prophet nor a fifth evangelist or a last Elias, nor a saint or holy man, still less the angel of the *Apocalypse*.

Arnold drew conclusions that must have rung in the ears of dominant Lutheran orthodoxy like a declaration of war: As Luther was not without his faults, he should not be taken as a universal teacher, nor should his teaching be made standard. Acknowledging his gifts and merits was one thing, taking his word as gospel was quite another. ' That it is human to err is apparent in his case too, on a number of important points in his books.' Far from exhausting the boundless ocean of truth and of God's mystery, he ventured opinions on the *Apocalypse* and St. James' Epistle that show ' how at the beginning he still had no sure understanding and foundation in a number of matters, and later through his great distress of spirit he lost something of his former candour and delight in the faith.' Thus Luther and his doctrine were robbed of their weight. Gottfried Arnold considered that acknowledgement of the truth, righteousness, and sound doctrine existed even apart from Luther; existed indeed even outside the Evangelical Church and even within the papacy.

(d) THE LUTHERAN CHURCH CRITICIZED

In short, Arnold had undermined the Lutheran orthodox church, founded as it was on implicit faith in Luther's doctrine.

Arnold pointed out on conscientious grounds that dependence on Luther meant depending on a man and robbing God of the honour due to him.

Orthodoxy felt itself threatened and became the relentless enemy of pietism. Arnold saw his views were not compatible with orthodoxy as it was, and set about summing it up from his own standpoint, in the very terms that Luther had used against papacy: men's work, men's teaching, constraint of conscience. Spener had largely prepared the ground for him.

He was able to appreciate Luther while rejecting Luther's church because individual inward piety (all that mattered) was present in Luther, but was remote from the regional church system of dogmatic Lutheranism.

The deficiencies of this church: first its unlucky birth. Luther wanted to give back to the parishes the rights the Pope had deprived them of. The parishes were in no position to turn themselves into independent bodies. ' Then civic authority took them over, place after place, and took with the parish the right to appoint the preacher, and so it has remained.' The result was that the parishes were excluded in the selection and naming of their preachers and the State had the direction of the churches. It would have been desirable ' if Luther had concerned himself with this and other matters to do with the welfare of the churches and had not trusted the *politicis* so much . . .'

Meanwhile the violation of the Church by the State worried him less than the violation of conscience by orthodoxy, with its so-called *Symbolical Books*. By what right were the theologians of the *Formula Concordiæ* in 1580 entitled to raise a collection of documents to the status of Symbolical Books?

His efforts concentrated on draining them of their dogmatic content. It ' cannot be denied that the true and only purpose of the *Augsburg Confession* and other books was to present and acknowledge the teaching and concepts which at that time the teachers and promoters of the Lutheran parishes supported and held to be true. By no means did these first witnesses remotely intend to bind their followers in the way that has actually occurred.' If Luther had foreseen such coercion of conscience and

the ensuing distress, he would never have put pen to paper again.
He frequently admitted and recognized that his own writings,
including these, were human, and therefore subject to mistakes
and errors. . . . Even less was it his intention to turn his catechisms, the greater and lesser, into symbols, as though he intended
them for any other purpose than the instruction of children and
simple people—as he himself wrote in the introduction to the
greater catechism. . . . Nor can proof be found elsewhere for
their authority, or for turning them into Symbolical Books
beyond what the few authors of the *Formula Concordiæ* had
to say.

He resented the Lutheran Church's State-establishment, its
misunderstanding of Luther, its non-Christian dogmatic consolidation, its formal ' papism.' On top of it all came a truly
piestistic complaint: that the evangelical spirit and holy conduct
were not only not to be found in the Lutheran Church but were
positively persecuted there.

Arnold did not stop short at the Bible itself. On historical
grounds he doubted the infallible validity of Holy Scripture in
its actual form; and on religious grounds he doubted that it was
meant to be taken literally. And if the traditional form and
authority of the Bible was to be questioned, logic required a
simultaneous denial of competence to councils and church
government, whether papistical or Evangelical. Arnold was
making headlong for boundless religious individualism. A man
was bound only to his own religious inwardness, in which Christ
revealed himself to him. Neither civic authority nor church
government could lay hands on it. When the latter imposed
codes of doctrine on a conscience, it was doing something in the
highest degree forbidden.

(e) PIETISM AND LUTHERANISM

Very remarkable was the way Arnold, questioning the whole
Lutheran church establishment and in fact any institutional
church whatever, could appeal to Luther for support. Two such
opposite attitudes as orthodoxy and pietism both drew material
for support from Luther: What a composite creature the

reformer was! It is equally remarkable that in casting loose from orthodoxy, Arnold gave almost exactly the same reasons as Luther used in cutting adrift from the Roman Catholic Church: freedom of conscience, together with the right not to be bound by man-made codes. A reformation time-bomb exploded in pietism.

Gottfried Arnold, preferring his Luther young, tried at the cost of Melanchthon and the Lutheran Church to win Luther for his side (an attempt Lessing repeated fifty and sixty years later). Luther was turned back into a normal human being with considerable flaws. Naturally this led to open conflict with the orthodox Lutheran Church, for whom the sacrosanct character of its founder was a matter of life and death.

Arnold's partiality for the first two centuries of Christianity was downright good Protestantism, and so in a general way was his contrasting of law and Gospel, merit and grace—except for the elimination of dogma. Out and out pietistic however was his habit of testing Christianity in whatever form he met it, to see if it was mystical and practical. He was less interested in a man's creed than in the intensity of his religious life. Not the right-thinking but the God-seeking man was the true Christian. And the barriers between confessions were of no importance.

The genuine Christian could not be hindered from attaining to union with Christ and achieving everlasting salvation merely by membership of the Roman or any other non-Lutheran church. In the introduction to his *Lives of the Faithful*, the remark occurs that under the papacy there had been people who with their whole heart sought God, and the reader could be assured of this because outwardly ' the true fruits of every tree . . . are tokens of the Holy Spirit dwelling within.' The inclusion of Catholics was justified, ' the universal invisible Church of Christ ' being ' in intention and condition ' what it is. On the other hand he passionately rejected all external forms of church and dogma, without regard for Catholic or Evangelical as such.

Arnold was giving religion an entirely new face. The important question on religion was no longer whether Catholic or Protestant, but whether inward and alive, or merely dogmatically prescribed. And beneath the surface a spiritual and intellectual revolution was taking place, the outcome of which informed the whole of modern times and in large part gave them their specific character. Inward or outward, spiritual or formal, subjective or objective religion: these terms now appeared as contradictory and mutually exclusive.

The result was a completely transformed Protestantism. Two mutually exclusive lines of thought were both called Protestant: one was Lutheran and dogmatic, the other turned away from dogma in favour of a free personal faith. Both groups continued to exist right into the twentieth century under the names of orthodox and liberal. Although mutually exclusive, each claimed Luther as its own, indebted to him for his doctrine on the one hand and on the other for the principles of freedom of conscience. Two genuinely Lutheran principles divided Evangelical Christianity beyond repair.

Pietism really was on many points the antithesis of orthodoxy, which found itself challenged on nearly all its main theses: a mystical moral Lutheranism opposed dogmatic Lutheranism; introspection and freedom of conscience stood over against doctrine; Christianity founded on the Word, firm in meaning, and on sacrament, against an individual ideal of ' being-Christian ' from the heart.

Instead of the invisible re-birth in faith, pietism demanded visible holy living. Where orthodoxy saw every deviation from doctrine as inspired by Satan, pietism considered it anti-Christian presumption for a confession to hold its doctrine as orthodox and alone right.

The broad lines of pietism are now clear. Its acute individualism was powerfully instrumental in bringing in the *Aufklärung*. The moment the Christian ethos and Christian piety made way for a rational moralism and purely moral piety, the age of enlightenment took the stage.

The outcome of pietism was, innately, Christian tolerance and, on a longer view, religious liberty (no more necessarily Christian). Goethe, as a young man, ardently reading Arnold's Church History, declared the latter to be the most important result of Arnold's activities. In the second book of *Wahrheit und Dichtung* he recounts his excitement in trying to form in his mind some idea of transcendental things. It was the time of his crisis and illness after his student years in Leipzig.

I came strongly under the influence of an important book [he wrote] which fell into my hands at the time, it was Arnold's *History of Churches and Heretics*. The man is not only a thoughtful historian, but at the same time full of piety and feeling. His sentiments were very much the same as mine, and what particularly delighted me in his work was the more advantageous picture of a number of heretics whom I had previously heard described as crazy and godless. The spirit of contradiction and pleasure in paradox lurks in all of us. I industriously studied the various points of view, and as I had often heard it said that at bottom everyone has his own religion, I found nothing more natural than that I too should put mine together, and I set about it with a great sense of well-being.

PART III
THE EIGHTEENTH CENTURY
THE AGE OF THE *AUFKLÄRUNG*

CHAPTER I

INTRODUCTION

THE eighteenth century took over a number of the ideas of the transition period of German Protestantism and brought them to fruition. But it was characteristic of it to take them out of their context and often give them a quite new meaning. They were removed from their Christian environment: their other-worldly focus and their biblical and Christian setting faded and they were firmly made to take root on the natural plane. The very words took on new meanings: ' providence ' came to be understood as ' purposeful world order,' and the concern for life hereafter grew dim and gave way to a concern for happiness and a state of general welfare in this world. God himself lost the *Tremendum Maiestatis* of his hold on men's minds, man no longer envisaged himself as creature imploring his Creator, but preferably as citizen of the world, paying respect to God as the wise director of it—all with an undertone of patronizing benevolence.

The transition period, wholly Christian, had accepted its stern Christian obligation: faith as a necessity and the whole of human life directed towards salvation in Christ. The eighteenth century shows how often pietistic ideas (Leibniz' and others) crop up in the general way of thinking and in the philosophies of state, history and humanity—but shows too what strange fruit the revolutionary seed sown in theology bore in due time.

Spener had declared Luther to be the bringer of freedom; Arnold declared, as a consequence of this freedom, that no one was bound to Luther. Leibniz called the Reformation an improvement, and if the improvement was considered incomplete and in need of furtherance, the idea of developing it was already there. But this concealed the fact that the Reformation in its own view had always meant something quite different, which was the restoration of Christian truth. Pietism considered that the Reformation had stopped short of its purpose and that it was a duty to carry it on. The *Aufklärung* took over this notion of improvement, originally conceived as an obligation with other-worldly resonances, gave it a secular, practical turn, and made of it the idea of *progress*: a typical eighteenth-century transmutation.

The transition period, though so wholly under the sign of *pietas*, meaning a personal Christian inward-turning and pious practices, had nonetheless seen Leibniz come out with his Christian universalism, independent of doctrine which was looked upon as an impediment rather than a necessary anchorage. In the eighteenth century, universalism, removed from its Christian context, emerged as cosmopolitanism and such ideas on humanity and human rights as were judged to be ' natural ' and ' reasonable.'

The laudable desire to climb over the fence of confession-alism, with Seckendorf preaching tolerance in the place of heresy-hunting, and Leibniz wanting to eliminate the differences by concentrating on general ideas held in common and on practical good works, stressing the primacy of love—this laudable desire to end a situation that was clearly non-Christian provoked attitudes and actions that were themselves, sometimes, non-Christian, or would become so. In the long run the confessions remained and the world they ruled over was secularized. Differ-ences of doctrine separated the confessions, and Seckendorf had wanted them to unite in so far as they held common doctrines. But the separation persisted, so the tendency was to cross the Rubicon, belittling dogma as the main obstacle—a process that slowly but surely asserted itself. Leibniz was not disinclined to hold certain dogmas for mere speculation. Spener disliked the literalness of church dogma as being insufficient, and this in-sufficiency struck Arnold as applying to the whole of doctrine. Pietism dissolved dogmatic Christianity into a Christianity of personal mysticism and personal morality.

What the relinquishing of dogma really entailed did not come to light until late in the eighteenth century, and the full conse-quences declared themselves only in the nineteenth and twentieth centuries. In dogma, regardless of confession, the main points of the Christian message (as each confession understood it) were gathered together into a body of doctrine. Thus, although the determination to forgo a dogmatic form of Christianity was made in an exemplary Christian spirit, nonetheless it constituted an impoverishment. The substitution of personal devotion, mystical experience, individual sensibility and reflection for dogmatic formulation could and did stimulate fresh religious life. But it depended more on individual personality than on the link with church and doctrine. Conscience was a more weighty factor than creed, and when they disagreed, it was considered, after Luther, to be Christian to heed conscience rather than creed. The ground was thus prepared for a Church-less Christianity. All forms of Christian orthodoxy, meaning belief established on an objective, super-personal level, were made suspect.

The personal ethical ideal came more and more into the foreground, gradually eclipsing a comprehension of the invisible (supernatural) effect of the sacraments. Spener's *Theological Considerations* already indicate distinct lines of thought which were to become decisive issues in the course of the eighteenth century; for instance, contrasting the *particular* Church and the Church proper; creed—and individual capacity for belief; public instruction in doctrine—and private religion.

Orthodoxy did not admit its defeat at the hands of pietism (for reasons which lay in its intrinsically Christian nature). It merely cut itself off from pietism and rationalism, returned to its sources, and took a firm stand on its original foundations.

The insistence of Lutheran orthodoxy on its right to exist has its place in a complete picture of the eighteenth century, and shall therefore occupy us for the space of a short chapter.

CHAPTER II

EIGHTEENTH-CENTURY ORTHODOXY

THE characteristic of orthodoxy in the eighteenth century is precisely the rejection of the new ideas of the transition period. It made no conscious concession to the spirit of the times. It continued to hold the same view of Luther, and the only change was the fresh alignment of forces: it was on the defensive as against pietism and 'enlightened' ideas on Luther. Hence a new stand and a harsher tone.

1. THE DEFENCE OF ORTHODOX LUTHERANISM

On April 28, 1716, a certain Moritz Wilhelm Wagner, otherwise unknown, held a disputation *sub præsidio Caspari Loescheri, sanctissimæ Theologiæ Doctoris*, on the theme: 'Luther as anti-pietist.' The author considered pietism in the light of the pure doctrine and accused the pietists of misunderstanding Luther, of taking his name in vain: 'They shout his name out into the world but fight against his doctrine and persecute it.'

The whole disputation was conducted from the standpoint that the pietists must be firmly separated from Luther, in fact they were to learn that their theology taught the exact opposite of Luther's. Wagner took a number of sentences from pietist writers, principally Spener, and refuted them by references to Luther's Galatian commentary. Thus he dealt with the claim that the validity of a church appointment depended on the worthiness of the person holding it; that all the ' re-born ' are entitled to preach and dispense the sacraments; and that the ' re-born ' were in a position to fulfil the laws of God. The very same claims, he said, had been refuted by Luther himself at the time of the Reformation. That the pietists dared to claim to be ' enlightened ' roused bitter wrath: 'We are not content with showing our own people that we do not oppress true piety, we are also compelled to tear down the others' mask of hypocritical piety.' The orthodox made much of their possession of the true doctrine of Wittenberg and a *pietas* in accord with God's word, teaching, practising and promoting the truth against the world, the flesh and devil. They had the audacity to assert that Luther had the pietists in mind when ' as a prophet alight from God ' he said:

> Of such zealots Germany has at this time *nota bene* a great many, with an immoderately good opinion of themselves which they wish godly, humble, learned, patient people to share, but who are, if the full truth were known, violent and poisonous hypocrites, wicked serpents and voracious wolves. . . . That they despise others and hold no one *nota bene* important but themselves is *nota bene* a sure sign that they seek neither Christ's honour nor the salvation of the people but only to be honoured and ceremoniously treated by everyone.

No doubt strict Lutheranism misunderstood pietism. But equally pietism misunderstood the necessity inherent in all religious activity for a firm foundation, a faith grounded in the Bible and set down in precise terms, if it is not to run amok and lose itself in phantasy, superstition, æstheticism, or downright paganism. Consciousness of this necessity was the heart and soul of orthodoxy. With religious individualism, and the consequent dissolution of creed and visible Church, it would have nothing to do. ' We depend not on Luther, not on Philipp, not on Chemnitz,' wrote Wagner, ' but on Christ alone. But: as Luther taught us the very same doctrine, . . . it is not inappropriate for us to love the name of Luther.' Here Wagner took up a position that strict Lutheranism always preconized, but in the eighteenth century the strongest expression was given it by Valentin Ernst Löscher, the Dresden Superintendent.

2. CHURCH HISTORY REVINDICATED
V. E. LÖSCHER

Löscher was in the main content with the seventeenth-century picture of Luther, with the doctrine in the centre and the more personal traits in the margin, but both as critic and defender he showed breadth and humanity. Without denying them, he considered it fruitless to dwell on Luther's faults, and concentrated his attention on the firm religious basis and Christian zeal of all Luther's actions. Unlike the pietists (and the later *Aufklärung*) he refrained from moral criticism.

> Heroic actions are performed neither for judgement nor for the imitation of lesser tempers. . . . Whereby it is to be remembered that a man who has not got Luther's heroic spirit should not follow his example further than the rule allows. . . . We can indeed forget the splinter [in Luther's eye] in comparison with the beam of his opponents'.

Löscher's point of view was the old Protestant one that Luther's doctrine coincided with the truth. Deviation from doctrine meant deviation from the truth. This view determined his Church history, and in this respect he was a late successor of Flacius Illyricus. There must be no political and philosophical afterthoughts where doctrine was concerned, it must stand firm as a rock, something of its very nature changeless.

This old-Protestant ethos inspired his attitude to pietism and the prevalent belief in progress: Lutheran doctrine, which contained, he believed, the whole of Christian truth, was the sole criterion for judging the history of Church and Reformation. Not piety, not striking personality, not intellectual quality, but how a man stood to ' the pure doctrine ' was decisive.

3. The Preservation of Lutheran Doctrine
V. E. Löscher

It is true that Lutheran orthodoxy cut itself off from the general development of ideas, but it succeeded by this means in safeguarding undiminished the whole body of Christian doctrine as contained in the *Augsburg Confession*, where non-orthodox religious and philosophical movements were gradually losing their Christian content.

So one should not condemn orthodoxy out of hand for its rigidity. The opposite of this rigidity (which moreover is better described as constancy, loyalty and obedience) is that changeability in belief preached and practised in the *Aufklärung* and subsequent movements, in the early classical period (Herder) and right into the general religious liberalism of the nineteenth and twentieth centuries, which thinned down the Christian atmosphere to an unbelievable degree and partly turned Christian doctrine into the opposite of what was intended in the Bible. This well-known state of affairs should be borne in mind and Christians should refrain from harsh criticism of orthodoxy; it made a whole-hearted stand against all that was destructive of faith. Its zeal for doctrine was basically and at best a real concern for salvation, and deserves respect as such. Everything depended on the doctrine remaining ' pure,' which it could only do if it remained true to Luther.

This must be clear if Löscher is to be understood. In the main it comes to this, he wrote, ' that we Evangelical Lutherans be still that same body which at the time of the Augsburg Confession were alone to profess it, and since then have adopted no new doctrine.' There is no difference between this and Johann Gerhard a hundred years earlier. But there is a change in method of approach: the Church is considered not only as to its nature but also historically. This may be due to lapse of time, or simply a reflection of the historical interests dominant since Leibniz, Seckendorf, Arnold.

The tolerant spirit of the eighteenth century also makes itself felt, if very slightly: Löscher recognized four stages in spiritual zeal in ' God's people.' The ' highest grade of zeal ' was to be applied against atheists and heathen, the next highest against those who despised the New Testament revelation: Jews, Turks, Naturalists; the third only against Christian heretics, and the fourth, the mildest, against the Protestant schismatics. And below this catalogue of zeals he wrote the admirable sentence: ' Zeal is directed against errors and not against persons, towards these the obligations of love apply.'

This confessionalism was milder in form, stricter in fact. In the main, Löscher with his sincere gravity remained without much response in his own day, the whole approach had become incomprehensible or at least unacceptable. Not princes and citizens only, even a number of Protestant theologians no longer understood.

CHAPTER III

TRANSITION THEOLOGY: JOHANN GEORG WALCH

JOHANN GEORG WALCH was born in 1693. He was first classical lecturer then professor of Theology (1724) at the university of Jena. His special interest was Church history. He edited Luther's works and wrote two five-volume ' Introductions ' to the theological controversies inside and outside the Lutheran Church. He added a Luther biography which was published in 1750–51. He was a contemporary of King Frederick William I of Prussia (1689–1740) and Johann Sebastian Bach (1685–1750), and was born like the latter in Thüringen which he loved to the end of his life. His work in Jena lasted over a half century and he died there at an advanced age in 1775.

He was a believing Protestant: what Luther taught was the truth, and to study it was to obtain the knowledge necessary for salvation and the glory of God. In his foreword in 1751, he said he had not been put off by the mass of existing literature on the subject from writing yet another Luther biography, ' for I saw I had much to complete, and here and there something to improve on, and that I could put the whole matter in better order.'

1. PRAGMATIC HISTORY

Walch was neither pietist nor strict orthodox. If he mentioned edification he insisted on information too, and on the ' outward circumstances ' as well as the ' inward circumstances.' In his *News of D. Martino Luthero*, in the place of an intensive study of the justification doctrine he said he intended to give all the information available: a quantitative rather than a qualitative statement.

The *Aufklärung* is responsible for a certain view of history which it called ' pragmatic.' Such a complete fusion of ideas occurred that 'pragmatic' came to be used instead of 'enlightened' in the general sense of *moderate*. 'Pragma' meaning 'object,' a pragmatic view of history originally meant an objective one. In the eighteenth century it entirely supplanted the theological view of history (which for Christian Europe began with Augustine and prevailed well into the seventeenth century, being responsible for works such as Bossuet's *Discours sur l'Histoire universelle*, 1681, right up to the end of the century).

But the general change in religious standpoint brought other changes too. In place of the Christian distinction, considered objective enough, between salvation and perdition, heaven and earth, sin and redemption, which coloured the older world history, we are given *subject matter*: the historical event as such. In Christian thought a point of view and a criterion are a *sine qua non*. But in pragmatic thought there was really only the 'matter,' from a 'matter of fact' point of view. Selection and the familiar perspective vanished, endeavour was directed to exhaustive documentation. Schröckh's 45-volume *Church History* which came out between 1768 and 1810, is a fine example of it. Pragmatic historians concerned themselves with ordering facts, tracing them back to their origins and deducing explanations, expatiating the while on the purpose and value of the historical method; they discovered lines of development pointing to the present, and found the whole unfolding of history demonstrably consonant with the intentions of a wise providence. It was important too to provide instruction for contemporaries and posterity. In eighteenth-century terms, they wrote for the benefit of humanity;—whereas the Christian historians wrote first and foremost for the honour of God. *Aufklärung* ideas predominated: use, purpose, progress, welfare, nature, humanity. There were new perspectives replacing the old ones, new topics replacing grace, redemption, perfectibility, salvation, heavenly Jerusalem and the communion of saints.

Walch, who was pragmatic in making his enumerations of 'external' and 'internal' matters as exhaustive as possible, was a thorough-going *aufklärer* in his rationalistic dissection of what was in effect organic and indivisible. He detached Luther's life from his Reformation, his ' gifts of nature and of grace ' from his ' merits,' his ' sanctified ' gifts of grace from the ' purely intellectual.' But he was a deeply believing Christian.

2. THE END OF THE LUTHER MYTH

Now the time has come to sketch in the picture of Luther which Johann Georg Walch and his method of scientific observation obtained from the sources. What he had to say of Luther's gifts constituted a dismissal of Lutheran orthodoxy: ' these gifts of nature and of grace . . . were in themselves ordinary gifts, only compared with other men they were bestowed on him in greater abundance. Extraordinary gifts we cannot ascribe to him, if we mean gifts not grounded in the natural powers of the man but going out over and beyond these.' As painstakingly as the seventeenth-century theologians stressing the supernatural character of Martin Luther's person and mission, this eighteenth-century theologian endeavoured to provide as ' natural ' an explanation as possible for the Reformation and its originator. Enlightened rationalism hated mystery and provided explanations satisfactory to reason for everything. It swept away—with much else—the remains of superstition and ungrounded over-naïve faith in authority still latent in the minds of the populace, and in the contemporary scholarship too. It was a healthy act and one which in many respects favoured a better understanding of Luther. But it heaped together superstition and mysticism, magic and authentic mystery, thus creating new confusion greater than before. ' If it pleases a man to see the Reformation as a miracle (*Wunder*) and to call it one, if he means an act in which God's might, wisdom and goodness were revealed in a special manner, no one endowed with understanding will find fault. It is not so absolutely unusual to use the word *Wunder* in this sense.'

These proceedings, secularizing the father of the Evangelical Church, were new and typical of the times. The great importance orthodoxy attached to his being the third Elias and the apocalyptical angel was depreciated by Walch, by ridding the terms of their strict biblical and compulsive sense: if used at all (which was inadvisable) they were merely an indication without obligation of Luther's remarkable piety, power and learning in divine matters. Walch recognized the occurrence of revelation and miracles, in the sense of a real breaking into the natural order, but only in the Bible. This was the hallmark of the early *Aufklärung*: it stopped short of Holy Scripture.

If not apocalyptical, Luther was truly great and sublime as scholar, orator, pious and bravely stalwart man of God. His gifts were appropriate ones from God destined for his mission: understanding, skill, virtue (all things the eighteenth century rated very highly). But the central problems Luther had so valiantly wrestled with were only mentioned in passing. Luther's main achievement was, it appeared, not the discovery of the doctrine of justification but the elimination of the authority of Rome. Walch's picture of Luther was to be a *natural* one, in contrast to the supernatural Luther of orthodoxy. No transformation but a real substitution, it lacked precisely those features which made Luther Luther in the eyes of the old Protestants.

3. Providence and Purpose

Walch combined his rationalistic view of history with a childlike faith in providence. The Reformation was a divine act because it was ruled and guided by providence, as evident from the concurrence of certain historical events.

It was the time . . . when the most important witnesses of the truth, Waldensians, Wiclifites, Hussites, had risen against the papacy and prepared the way for the Reformation. The measure of papal wickedness was full . . . and for a long time people had been longing for an improvement of the Church. . . . Sciences, schools, academies, book-printing for the rapid dissemination of the Gospel not only by word of mouth but also in writing on paper, . . . all were important. . . . And this was no accident: God of his goodness and wisdom ordained things in such a way that whatever was required for the spread and acceptance of the truth which the Reformation was to bring into the light again, was provided.

Likewise the efficacy of providence was clearly evident:

> In former times a variety of people wanted to bring about an improvement of the Church and even wanted to set to work on it. They were however unable to carry it through because God had not selected them as instruments; the time appointed by him had not yet come. But it all made a good beginning with Luther and its further course was blessed.

An important and remarkable argument was the following: Luther did not specially intend a Reformation, and the quarrel with Tetzel over the indulgence was more a private matter.

> If this difference of opinion had been a mere human act, how soon it would have been solved and the controversy settled. But the hand of the Lord was engaged and—a fact that ought to be more often brought to light—the pope was struck blind and Luther was driven by power from on high to go through with that which he had begun.

No Christian theologian, no one with a sense of history, would dream of denying that world events are under God's providence. But a line has to be drawn at linking providence with definite intentions, for we cannot tell what it was God intended with Christians and non-Christians, Luther and Reformation. We can at best believe in all faith that he has a purpose in them all, more not. (And that at the last his will is love.) But the detailed reading of God's intentions in history was a hobby of the *Aufklärung*, which saw God's providence as a rational and wise plan which one could work out afterwards and put to the test for its wisdom and goodness. There was no sense of awe in the presence of the *Mysterium tremendum*.

4. THE RELATION OF STATE AND RELIGION

Evangelical religion was put to the same test as providence. The stress was on how far it was practical, moral and natural. Its function was to be useful in moral life and in the State. At the same time the view that Protestantism contained the truth and was necessary to salvation was not contested. The Christian *aufklärer* saw Salvation and State as other-worldly and worldly values united in Lutheran Protestantism. A falling off from Protestantism meant perdition in the religious sense and imprudence in the political sense—both at once.

> Any prince who turns from the Protestant Church to the Catholic is not only acting against God and his conscience, denying the truth and hurling his soul into everlasting damnation . . . he is also offending against all State prudence. He lets himself be limited in his powers and forfeits many rights he hitherto possessed.

Roundly, ' the Roman religion is harmful to the civic State.' All its institutions confirmed this. Its church service:

> The constraint of conscience is here so great that as history shows, and particularly the wars of religion, it can give rise to the greatest confusion and disorder in civic society. In the papacy far too many days are holy days . . . whereby subjects are kept away from their work without cause and led into idleness and other vices.

Its monasteries:

> It often looks as though a republic has more harm than use from these. The great riches of certain monasteries were best given to the State for the support of certain subjects: but as it is, they often serve merely for the maintenance of people who spend their time in idleness, in sin and vice . . .

And above all celibacy:

> . . . seen quite rightly as one of the most statesmanly strokes of the Roman Church, and in consequence as a thing of decisive disadvantage to civic society. Church properties are thus held together and it is not so easy to obtain that they be put to good use. . . . The religious are by this means easily kept in a state of reverence and obedience towards the pope; for on the other hand if they had wife and children they would be more concerned with these than with church affairs, and would turn to the authority in the district in which they

lived, and from whom they could expect support for their families after their death, and would thus lose a good deal of their zeal for the honour and exaltation of the pope.

It was implicitly assumed that Catholic doctrine was false, but the view commonly taken was that it was harmful to the State and to civic society. Here again Walch's method contained profoundly non-Christian seeds. He expected religion to measure itself by the State. This could well become monstrous and give rise to appalling distortions—and indeed did so in the course of the next two hundred years. Nonetheless it was as a result of considering the uses and disadvantages of religion to the State that Johann Georg Walch gave his unqualified approval to Martin Luther's reformation. 'The attitude of our religion to the civic State is a very different one. It is completely consonant with it and with its true interests.' Luther's great merit was his teaching on public authority and the preaching of the obedience due to it, with the consequent obliteration of papal church rule. Walch called upon the ' great lords ' to thank God most heartily for what happened to them and to their estate through Luther. He meant the institution of the princely episcopacy, by means of which princes ' attained to their fully highest power in their own states, which is no mean benefit bestowed on them by God'; the restoration of the status and rights of rulers—' theirs by reason and law'; the instruction of subjects that honour is due to rulers in God's stead, in so far as compatible with divine law and conscience; the secularization of church property or its allocation ' to better uses '; and it was also a merit of Luther's that he placed princes in a position ' to lead a quiet and peaceful life with their subjects without papal disturbance and oppression . . . and to take much better care of the spiritual and bodily welfare of their subjects.'

In short, a religion is good and acceptable in the degree of its compatibility with the existing form of State. True, there was a conscience clause. And Luther had been improved upon: Luther taught after St. Paul that man must be subject to authority, for all authority is from God; Walch required them to honour authority in God's stead. He probably meant well, and felt that the conscience clause settled the matter. In fact, however, he was taking a fatal step, whether he knew it or not. Honour civic authority in God's stead, and the State (later, the nation) grows into a religious entity (and turns itself into God). The coupling of religion with the functions of civic society and the absolute State, which had started in the Reformation period, was continued by the *Aufklärung*, which saw the Church as foe of the State wherever it had power of its own, and rejected it in its Catholic form because it cut across the ' freedom' of the State in its episcopal function. Luther by his Reformation had rid the Church of its power-potential and the Reformation was on that account meritorious, useful or progressive.[1] The idea can be traced through Frederick the Great and Justus Möser to the popular late *aufklärer* of the turn of the nineteenth century. The precedence given to State and society over Church, blindness to the value of contemplation in religious life, this and much else show how far with Walch a secular point of view had penetrated right into the heart of theology. Hallmarks of enlightened theology, in Walch personally they were combined with a staunch Lutheran faith; but later-comers discovered the incompatibility of this faith with the principles of enlightened thought, and proceeded to strip the faith of its orthodoxy and to transform it into a humanly comprehensible and ' reasonable' devotional attitude. One of the most significant of these was Johann Salomo Semler, born in 1725, whom we shall study in the next chapter.

[1] Cf. the wholly opposite opinion of Spener. That the will to turn the Church into a State institution grew powerful among the rulers of the Catholic lands of Europe (e.g., Austria, Bavaria) in those days is well known. But two Protestant characteristics are lacking in the Catholic position: the State Church system as a by-product of the Reformation, and a favourable estimation of the Reformation for having helped to bring the State Church system into existence. Remains the dogmatic and canonical majesty of the Pope.

CHAPTER IV

CRITICAL THEOLOGY OF THE *AUFKLÄRUNG:* JOHANN SALOMO SEMLER: DECLARATION OF INDEPENDENCE

JOHANN SALOMO SEMLER (1725–1791) was born in a Saalfeld parsonage. He was extremely industrious all his life as his 200 written works go to show. From 1752 he taught theology in Halle and continued teaching it until his death in 1791.

He was the father of the modern, so-called historical, Bible criticism which dominated all nineteenth-century Evangelical theology. In fact he completed the transition from the dogmatic to the scientific study of the canonical books, especially the New Testament, treating them not as inspired revelation but as historical documents available for research and yielding information on their authors, their relations to one another and their place in history. He came to the conclusion that much in the canonical books was accidental, contingent and purely local in interest, without dogmatic value. The real validity of scripture he saw in the passages that contributed to a man's spiritual formation.

1. LUTHER, THE AUTHOR OF INDEPENDENCE

More critical and more personal in his Luther portrait than Walch, Semler took up his own standpoint and discussed Luther from it. He saw the Reformation as a movement through which humanity freed itself from the shackles of dogma and church, and piety and scholarship expanded.

True discipleship of Luther consisted, for Semler, not in teaching his word and repeating his views on Schwenckfeld and Zwingli, but in competing with him in fervour of prayer, conviction and 'intercourse with God.' He was one with the pietists in stressing inwardness and individuality; the man was important rather than the matter, in fact he neglected the latter entirely if we mean salvation and the purity of doctrine in the strict old-Protestant sense.

In Bossuet's *Histoire des Variations des Églises protestantes* (1688) the Protestants were accused of not holding to their own doctrines —an accusation that no longer made sense in *Aufklärung* theology. Semler replied:

The Bishop should have shown the real advantage of Luther; apart from freedom from episcopal vexations, he gave every Christian the freedom to think for himself about Christian ideas and truths and to follow his conscience; thus he changed the former Latin ideas of penance, faith, justification, good works, etc., and everyone could follow his line of thought for himself. This is necessarily much more desirable than the old tales they used to harp on, and the obligation to believe what the Church believed in Latin, by order of the inquisitors. I said everyone was now glad to take part in thinking and discussing—formerly to all intents and purposes the privilege of the Clericorum.

Two lines further on he added:

It is no small matter that Luther very soon, immediately after the Bull of Pope Leo, 1520, declared his and his friends' independence from the Pope. Thus I explained the freedom which Luther gained to elucidate the words of consecration, as meaning transubstantiation or not—retaining the substance of the bread. That Bossuet accuses him of variations is only to his mind worth mentioning; for other Christians who have no such principles of unchangeability of doctrine and opinion, it is sheer waste of time; a set view on this point is no part of general instruction in the faith, but concerns the particular teaching of individual churches, which need to establish the external association of their many members in one church society. . . . Nonetheless I readily granted all the faults and exaggerations in Luther to which attention was drawn, and have myself read out the vehement raw passages in the pamphlets against King Henry VIII . . . in order the better to counteract another form of exaggeration in which many people indulge, taking it all for holy zeal and even a sign of the presence of God's spirit; I found this crusty taking sides very disagreeable. . . . Also, however much others may praise the fact that Luther married when he was already forty-one years old, I whole-heartedly supported Erasmus and others who held that he deserved strong censure for such a step; but I observed how in similar situations we all do exactly the same, willy-nilly, for now as then, *optimus ille est, qui minimis urgetur vitiis*. Without faults, without quite definite faults Luther was not capable of so much, was not capable of undertaking such great things, why not admit it? His bouts of self-exaltation, for instance in the silly squabble with Zwingli as to who began it, I could not overlook; nor the conceitedness of his views on the effects of his anti-papal writing; for I could find no noble sublime effects; on the civic plane they were badly needed and very welcome; but the new holy moral order of mankind I could not find. Such effects as there were, were not at all unexpected ones, nor did they cost exorbitant pains. And then I thought the more, how often Luther complained of the bad fruits of the evangelium; if he held that they were his concern alone, and the Roman and Swiss churches had no true Christian religion, he was gravely wrong. But I cannot blame him, however over-hasty and vehement he was, he knew what he knew, and knew too how inevitably everything depends on circumstances . . . changes in point of view were matters of personal experience. I considered he might have taken such a strong line in opposing other views precisely because he was blamed for the existence of so many views, which, according to the old principles of unity of faith and church, was both abominable and offensive.

We are familiar with the complaint about Luther's personal deficiencies: with or without reservations it sounded down the centuries. With admirable clarity Semler pointed out what seemed to him the positive achievement of the Reformation: it was *freedom*, and was due to Luther for the stand he made on its behalf.

Freedom was twofold: outwardly, freedom from constraint and oppression from the doctrinal Church; from its ' vexations '; inwardly, freedom of thought and conscience.

Here is the new eighteenth-century Luther: the reformer as bringer of freedom.

Doctrine and dogma as such were no longer in the picture. We know that Luther never thought of them as purely formal, without content; on the contrary, their content was binding and saving. Of its very nature, doctrine, like truth, had to be invariable and final. But Semler taught the opposite, doctrine was ' inevitably local,' that is, necessarily limited, not intended for all men at all times; and 'variable,' that is, not downright binding. He went into some detail. Pushing aside Luther's focal teaching on man's lack of free will, reducing dogma to a mere formula, he left little scope for the ' confessions,' none of which could now claim that its message as such was Christian truth. If dogma was but a variable formula, Christian truth was elsewhere, if anywhere at all. The pietists said it lay in the heart when lit by inner light; Semler said more soberly, ' in the good idea of use to all Christians.' The inner light and the good idea could be present in any Christian, independently of his membership of a particular confession, and it appeared to Semler very unjust to say that the non-Lutheran churches had ' no true Christian religion.'

What issued from the view that doctrine is only relative was *tolerance*. We are astonished at how parallel the lines are along which Arnold's, Spener's and Semler's thoughts ran. Pietism left its trace deep in the German *Aufklärung*, but unlike pietism, the *Aufklärung* stood for the maintenance of the official regional churches and public instruction in religion. It was in keeping with its love of order and systematization, and the sympathetic eye it kept on the interests of the sovereign state. Semler gave a practical explanation for the continued existence of confession and doctrine: though deprived of their original functions, they served to join their adherents outwardly in a visible ' church society.' Doctrine was thus debased to a code for the ordering of a religious communion from outside.

' I thought infallibility was not to be looked for in Luther or other Protestants, as we were not prepared to let the Pope have it.' In so far as Luther might, in his circumstances, be right, others like Zwingli, Carlstadt, Schwenckfeld might be right too. Thus a Christian did not necessarily have to be Lutheran at all. And yet it is common knowledge that Luther preferred to break with the Swiss rather than yield a single letter of his Lord's Supper teaching. ' That particular notion of Luther's,' said Semler, ' need not be reckoned as part of the Christian faith that binds all Christians together.'

In spite of the fact that Luther, as Semler could not conceal, had spoken of his doctrine as ' necessary for salvation,' and called down damnation on all deviation—said Semler, he really knew it was conditional and limited, and only expressed himself so strongly because of the still prevalent tendency to find unity necessary, inherited from the old Church; and had over-stated his case to keep the masses from self-reformation and counteract the danger of confusion in public life.

Aufklärung theology had a decided preference for ideas that were easily understood and accessible to rational arguments. Every question had the right to a straight and candid answer. Why did Luther need freedom? Because the constraint and tyranny of the old Church had become unbearable. Then why did he allow his own Church powers of coercion? Out of consideration for the masses, to keep them quiet. What else was Luther's due, and what to him had seemed important, were questions that were not raised. And what induced the intrinsically problematical establishment of Church and doctrine—namely his conviction of the saving nature of the justification doctrine—was simply not grasped. There was a complete lack of any understanding for Luther in his real depths and in his religious uniqueness. It was no longer clear why he was the decisive figure in Protestant Christianity. The *Aufklärung* saw him as one among others, though still formidable. Semler had no mind for special and extraordinary gifts of grace, and reduced Luther's place in history and in theological achievement to a purely relative one.

2. THE REFORMATION AS INDIVIDUAL REVOLUTION

(a) HISTORY AND PROVIDENCE

The scientific method of historical studies had completely ousted the dogmatic method. But Semler and Walch saw the course of history as lit up by religious moments (religious in the 'enlightened' sense). For Semler, the Reformation arose out of ' human and indeed comprehensible occasions ' and was no ' miraculous event,' it was a revolution which could be understood by insight into the general history of the time. But it was quite appropriate

> to describe that revolution as a great benefit of God's and constantly to exhort Protestants to due thanksgiving and praise of God and more confidence in his rule. For myself at least God and God's providence in the human world are no empty words. The fact that numbers of people have indeed made bad and unjust use of this benefit, and have even turned it to evil purposes, made me the more conscious of our indebtedness, and the need always to have God's great plan in mind.

Semler did not say outright that he meant by God's ' plan,' humanity on the road to eternal salvation, through faith in Christ. Presumably that was not what was in his mind at all; but rather, the development of mankind to a higher stage through intellectual and material progress (in fact enlightenment, *Aufklärung*) as his contemporary Gotthold Ephraim Lessing proclaimed it in his *Education of the Human Race*.

(b) THE REFORMATION—HISTORICAL BACKGROUND

' I held that the seed of that revolution had germinated for almost a hundred years, starting principally in the history of the previous, fifteenth, century.' There were two main pre-suppositions: one, that the Pope was already known to be a purely political power and an unjust steward. The other, that since the Councils of Constance and Basel, 'much real light' had been shed ' on the German world.'

Book-printing provided an effective measure against ignorance and the old privileges of the Church, and the spread of education was a potent challenge to the sterile theology of the day. Semler dared to say that Valla, Cusanus, Johann von Wessel, Pico della Mirandola, Erasmus and a number of others, not excepting the late mediæval mystics, 'had already perceived all the truths that were opposed to the general unsound Church religion, and expressed them candidly.' He concluded from this ' that neither Zwingli nor Luther discovered a single wholly new proposition or leading idea.' The spread of learning (to which the Greek-Latin editions of the New Testament belonged together with their German translation) had, it was assumed, as a natural consequence, the decline of the old Church in power and authority. For the New Testament made it clear ' to many thousands of readers' that the universal official Church had nothing to do with ' private religion,' that is, with individual personal piety, for ' they wanted to put the Pope and the Church in God's place and not to reflect for themselves.'

The late mediæval papacy was painted ultra-black.

> For us it is enough [wrote Semler] to learn to know the horrid opinions, the accursed wickedness of the then leader and servant of that old Church; . . . the constant tyranny of its orthodoxy, the abomination of which surpasses all that is told of a Nero, Diocletian, etc., in olden times. That anti-Christian spirit and the attendant misfortune of human society one must learn to know aright, if one . . . would know why Luther behaved as he did and finally desired, *deus vos impleat odio papæ*. . . .

It is characteristic of Semler and his time that the papacy was hardly ever accused of false doctrine, it was its supposed despotism and moral corruption that aroused indignation. Papal power he described as ' the unworthy means by which that rotten religion . . . stood in the way of godly Christian freedom and the conscientious application of a man's own wholesome perceptions.' He disapproved of ecclesiastical prescriptions, ' un-Christian man-made codes' chiefly because they 'do nothing to promote . . . private religion.'

(c) CHARACTERISTICS OF THE REFORMATION

(i) *Private religion versus ecclesiastical constraint*

A mighty universal current, intellectual, religious, scientific, and not least, political, in nature, that undermined the existing ecclesiastical order; desire for freedom breaking down all barriers; individual piety refusing to be disturbed by the Church in its devotions and its ' salutary' perceptions: when this com-bined process had reached ripening-point, the Reformation broke out. Luther's special contribution was, it appeared, to lead it to victory and demolish the old order.

> The thing was not to be stopped; it would have happened to a greater or lesser degree even if Luther had indulged in no further outbursts against the Pope. . . . More than a thousand heads and hands were already at work, independently of Luther. . . . When Luther offered to keep silent about his opposition to Pope and Emperor, he knew well enough that the free upward surge of individual religion in contempt of the so faulty outward Church could now no more be suppressed either by the stake or by imprisonment. . . . I believed I was convinced that even if Luther had died on the spot or been handed over to the Pope, a reformation . . . would never-theless have proceeded on its course quite satisfactorily. . . . So Luther actually did little; but a very great deal occurred.

Semler went a whole step further than Walch, who held that Luther was equipped by God with special gifts of learning, courage and eloquence, to help him guide the Reformation to a successful outcome. For Semler this was quite unnecessary. Luther had set the pace, it is true, but the freedom movement was ready to go ahead whether Luther took part or not. The

purpose of the Reformation was not to preach the Lutheran
doctrine of justification but to proclaim freedom of the spirit
and private religion; also to improve morals when the chief
blow had been dealt and the papal yoke removed.

(ii) *Intellectual, political and moral revolution*

The Reformation was also a revolution destined to effect a
threefold transformation of the Church: intellectual, political,
moral. The first was over: freedom of thought and religious
conviction had won the day. The second was over: in all
Protestant lands the regional church system, free of the Pope,
had adapted itself to the local form of rule. The third, the
moral revolution, was not wholly completed: ' the new
holy order of humanity, no longer in fear of papal dictates,
I did not see.'

Improvement was possible: the *Aufklärung* felt it had a
mission to continue the work of the Reformation. And on
another point the Reformation had only made a start: ' doctrine '
stood in constant need of perfecting. Not the justification
doctrine, for which Semler showed little interest, nor any other
established dogma; the entire body of theology was to be
brought back to basic Christian principles, reformulated in such
a way that, while outwardly uniting all individual members of
a regional church to their spiritual enrichment, it would permit
the unmolested expansion of private religious life. This he saw
as the function of all the ordinances which, since Luther's Church
ordinances in Wittenberg and Bugenhagen's for the great lower-
German cities, had appeared in large numbers in the various
Evangelical districts, provinces, cities and states. Where
ordinances are concerned, one must, said Semler, proceed from
this principle: ' To start with, only the main purpose need be
achieved; the rest will be improved on occasion by judicious
Christians of their own accord.' Improvements would be adapted
to the requirements of time and place, and Luther was called to
witness that ' much room must be left to the spirit of Christian
freedom.'

(iii) *A stage in the progress of humanity*

This new dynamic conception of the Reformation stood in stark opposition to the older dogmatic conception. For old Lutheran theology, it was a singular saving event; for *Aufklärung* theology, a stage in the intellectual and religious progress of humanity.

The end result for Semler was freedom in theological interpretation, conscientiousness in research and religious devotion, and—as against papal orthodoxy—a perception[1] of the perfectibility of doctrine and Church constantly striven for, never fully achieved. Nonetheless he had no hesitation in calling the whole transformation of the Church by the older Protestants, from Melanchthon to Walch, a godly work. 'It will verily be and remain a work of God, and will increasingly prove its worth as such in its continuation, which is all part of it.' But this was only verbal accord, what he meant by tradition was in direct contradiction to what the old Protestants meant. Having called the Reformation a godly work, he went straight on to say that as men had produced it, it bore the stamp of humanity and insufficiency. It is not difficult to ascribe a godly character as understood by Semler, to all historical events of which we approve. 'It is sheer vanity to make a special point of the purely godly side of those events, a godliness which all others have to do without, in order that we alone may be endowed with it.'

While the course of history as such is attributed to divine guidance, the special individual event loses its soul-saving character. The idea of godliness loses its old precise Christian content, in the same way as providence and doctrine. In Semler contexts godliness means something like 'progress in history,' the forerunner of what Herder and Hegel later maintained to be the connection between history and God.

Everything new he had said about the Reformation Semler termed—in contrast to orthodoxy—a reasonable and lenient way

[1] ' This is the Lutheran principle, that we should deduce all doctrine from Holy Scripture as well as we are able to do so; that is to say, grow and increase in it. Precisely an unchangeable doctrine would be a former papal principle ' —Semler.

of thinking, by which he meant, as a man of his time, that 'without doubt it is far more suitable for instruction and for the guidance of one's own understanding than the condemnations in vogue [in former days].'

3. FREEDOM OF CONSCIENCE—RELIGIOUS SUBJECTIVITY

The Lutheran conscience in its new aspect, which was responsible for Semler's 'lenient' way of thinking about the Reformation, proved a bold and powerful foe of orthodox tradition, and did not belie its origins in pietism. Freedom of conscience in the sense of freedom in conviction, thinking and teaching, also in the expounding of Scripture, marked all Semler's work, his Bible studies were affected, and his students were told to adopt the same principle. All this was contrary to the theological tradition in which he had been brought up and educated, and he was not easy in his mind when he broke with the past. He believed, however, that he had hold of an authentic legacy of the Reformation, and at the age of 55 he remarked, in the second volume of his autobiography:

As we no longer wished to be subject to such unreasonable Church regimentation [meaning the papacy] of necessity we altered the Church canon, and neither Luther nor Calvin, even had their previous conscience desired it, could have prevented thoughtful Christians from culling from this Protestant Bible whatever was for them best and most useful; without first asking for permission from the preachers and theologians. If many, including theologians, thought otherwise and so taught, they were following their own conscience; but they cannot insist that private Christians must keep to a particular kind of conscience or cease to call themselves Lutherans. This consideration, which I jotted down time and again on odd slips of paper and in the margins of books, has cost me much anxiety and disquiet.

The consequences were immense. Unrestricted freedom of personal conviction gave rise to unrestricted religious subjectivity and to relativism. The only restraint still in existence was in effect no genuine one, Semler meant by it rulers and civic authorities. But what powers did he allocate to the State? The right to give the universities prescriptions on the ' maintenance of the principles of freedom of religion '; to lay down ordinances for preaching and teaching; and to maintain or alter them at discretion; to use their influence in ' the prevention of public disturbances on account of religion.' Taken all in all, merely a State-run Church police, nothing to do with the religious direction of subjects. Semler intended only the ' external ordinances ' of the authorities ' of which the immediate application is also external'; namely 'the quiet and order of Church society.' Therefore, apart from the ecclesiastical function of public authority, nothing remained to provide a brake for unbridled religious subjectivity. Each single Christian, Semler always insisted, had freedom of thought and enquiry, the right to a private ' inner ' religion, and was on religious ground in so far autonomous that no church and no theology was empowered to order what he should think in matters of faith.

This was *relativism* in its application of freedom of conscience to the subject matter of dogmatics. Luther's formulation of the Lord's Supper doctrine (or the doctrine of justification or any other doctrine) was, he said, merely the expression of his private conviction. It was his good right as a Christian to have his private views, and no one should contest it. But when he wanted to impose his personal conviction on others, then he was infringing the right of conscience and behaving in an un-Christian way; still more so, when he publicly condemned other people's private opinions for differing from his own. Truth as expounded by any Christian confession was essentially relative. We know how deeply this view has penetrated into the religious consciousness of modern Christendom. ' No single Christian party has alone the whole truth; none has all falsehood or has totally departed from the foundation of Christianity.'

4. INTOLERANCE, TOLERANCE AND RELATIVISM

Semler's attitude appears as a judicious, reasonable and mild departure from the combative intolerance and harshness of orthodoxy, strong and virile in its intolerance because it believed it was in possession of the truth. In the northern and central German universities, Lutheran intolerance was taught until the middle of the eighteenth century. Semler reports that university preachers and teachers accepted as normal 'the daily consequences and conclusions' to the effect 'that other forms of doctrine—whether of real Lutheran teachers, or, more still, of the Reformed (Calvinists), the Roman Catholics, and the Socinian writers—undermined the very foundations of faith and salvation and therefore no one could be saved but a properly strict Lutheran.'

Semler described it as a crude spirit of polemics, meretricious, harmful, poisonous in nature, un-Christian, unjust, inhuman in attitude; and the damnations the Protestants distributed to all and sundry he termed, human means to a human end, bereft of any claim to godliness and as worthless as papal anathemata. The squabbling preachers only upset people and 'promoted or facilitated un-Christian living.' Calov, the teacher of dogmatics, instead of raising the hue and cry on account of Socinus' liberality in not denying salvation to Calvinists, Arians and Anabaptists, would do better to refute the statement of this same Socinus excluding Catholics from everlasting salvation.

Semler disliked most of all in this oppressive one-sidedness and narrowness the hampering effect on science and its free expansion. He condemned the dogmatic consolidation of doctrine in the sixteenth century, and above all the *Formula Concordiæ*, and lamented the damage done: 'individual research and learning have so little encouragement among us'; the cause was not only the dogmatic stranglehold but also human weakness: 'True scholarship died out everywhere, for it was so easy now to be a popular teacher, pure and simple.'

In his autobiography he gives an account of his own struggle for freedom:

As the Christian parties passed sentence one upon another as though each alone advanced on God's right hand, [there spread among them as it were a] conscientious legalised hatred

. . . which I also for some length of time bore against other parties, as one of the obligations of a teacher of the Lutheran Church. . . . I was often not a little confused . . . at having to explain that the reasons and answers it was customary to proffer against Roman, Reformed or Socinian theology were not of a kind to provide evidence of unconscientious . . . and un-Christian notions worthy of damnation, in the Roman or Socinian teacher. . . . This I must admit: the more earnestly I desired to pursue the right policy, the more by dint of intensive reading I came to take a non-party view of the way to expound Scripture. I came to see that a true sense of conviction and inner religion can be at heart the same in all Christian parties, however much modes of speech and scholars' and theologians' jargon might differ.

There is another relevant passage where he touched on the contrast between the Lutheran and Zwinglian doctrine of the Lord's Supper. He admitted the differences but stated that differences of ' presentation ' were unimportant for Christians. For both doctrines ' promoted,' one no worse than the other, both in a Christian manner, ' the whole purpose and true value of the Lord's Supper.'

That was tolerance as Semler understood it: respect for the religious conviction of the other man and horror of all constraint in the name of religion. Moreover Christianity consisted in a true sense of conviction and inner religion, characteristics observable in all Christian parties, and even alike in all, so there was no reason for conflict at all. How the balance had shifted since the sixteenth and seventeenth centuries! It was no longer a matter of *what* one believed, but *how* one believed. Conscientiousness was the criterion, not the object of one's belief. Not whether the content of doctrine were true, but whether views on it were presented in a beneficial and useful manner. Consequently Semler enquired of Roman and Socinian theologians, not whether their doctrine agreed with Scripture, but whether their attitude were conscientious and Christian.

In all this he shows more eighteenth-century than Christian

affiliations. Universal Christian tolerance was an idea that went more than half way towards Christian indifferentism and a purely human and rational conception of humanity. How the idea of tolerance connects with the endeavours of absolutist rulers to form their subjects into more or less coherent orders is familiar enough in political history. Here and there before the French Revolution, and universally after it, religious tolerance became as a matter of course the basis of the constitutions of European states.

Semler's tolerance goes back to a temperament far more closely affiliated to Goethe with his belief in polarity than to Luther's stormy religious upheavals. He deduced from his own thesis of freedom of enquiry that he should not base his studies on those of other scholars; on the other hand, ' other contemporaries might prefer the contrary, according to the rules, and be very unsatisfied with my work,' and that he considered to be quite in order, and put on record his reason; to the naturalistic thinking of his day it must have seemed immensely evident: ' —for in the moral and Christian world God intended to have forces straining against one another, just as they inevitably do in the physical world.'

In other passages he makes a present to future liberalism of a formula which has continued in use to our own day, by justifying tolerance on grounds of temperament, with the unintentionally pungent sentence: ' Whoever wishes for the spread of religion and morality must above all not hinder their diversity.'

5. CHURCH AND RELIGION

THE VISIBLE AND THE INVISIBLE CHURCH

Semler was a member of the Lutheran Church and described himself all his life as a Lutheran teacher. He distinguished very exactly between ' Luther's mode of speech . . . which discloses Luther's personal way of thinking,' and the first principles of the Lutheran Church. By Luther's mode of speech, or presentation, he did not only mean the familiar quotations, but also quite basic doctrines which used to possess dogmatic validity. By

principles of the Lutheran Church he meant in the first place
the freedom of theological research and religious conviction;
and for the rest it belonged to the nature of the Lutheran and
indeed all Protestant churches not to become committed to any
invariable doctrines but to look to their alteration, growth and
improvement according to the circumstances of time and place.
There was a negative element not to be omitted: the Lutheran
Church was ' opposed to the papacy from the beginning.'

Accordingly the Church of Luther is a community based on
a religious attitude to life—hardly even a community in the
sense of sharing a common attitude to a coherent religious
conception: ' The more the first principles of the Protestant
Churches safeguard for every single man his freedom of individual
thought and enquiry, as against the former papistical system of
doctrine, so that he can decide within his own conscience: the
dearer these principles will be to me.'

Churches were held together from outside by the doctrine
valid in the respective regional church systems and by ordinance
of authority; that is, by State and theology, intimately linked.
The external unity of a regional church or churches would not
be disturbed if the individual theologians represented ' quite
contrary opinions ' on canon, inspiration, and other theological
concerns, and taught matter varying from one to the other:
it was permissible—not because a Christian dogma was available,
giving play enough for various interpretations and only prevent-
ing the spread of excrescences (there was no such dogma), but
because unity would be maintained by the theologians with their
contradictory opinions, who ' still remain united as true conscientious pastors of their parishes, because their final purpose is
the same.' Thus the unity of the Church lay not in the unity of
doctrine but in a common purpose; not a concrete one, it must
remain subjective: not everlasting salvation, but a sense of
conviction and the integrity of individual Church members,
together with an activity in keeping with their religious attitude.
Wide new horizons were opening out.

Beyond the confessions there was, Semler tried to prove, a
true community of all Christians: one single invisible universal

Church. 'The particular Church doctrines,' he said, 'only distinguish individual groups according to outward rights and competences, on account of the outward final purpose: the securing of quiet and order; but they do not actually separate true Christians from one another in regard to inner religion, even when outwardly they form quite a variety of groups each with its own doctrinal books.' The exaltation of the invisible inner Church over the outward visible Church was absolute. Its members were of quite another, higher, quality. Any individual could be a member of the ' outward group or party ' by mere outward ' conformity.' But to be a true Christian and member of the invisible community, mere conforming membership was not enough—' only genuine inwardness, lively spiritual experience.' As steady ' growth in insight into the content of truth and its uses ' was fundamental to Semler, complete likeness and agreement could never come about ' even among the most honest and truest Christians.' The unity of the invisible Church was not affected by this diversity, for it was founded on and bound together by the ' unity of spirit and affinity of motions in such different dispositions.' Semler was fond of repeating how the real invisible Church was the communion of ' true Christians.' Where inner religion, a truly Christian sense of conviction, harmony of innermost motions, views, principles and perceptions existed, then Christians came together easily, ' united at heart; and this spiritual union can be disturbed by no symbolical books.'

What distinguished the members of the invisible Church was inner or true spiritual religion, and what this religion consisted in, was not Semler's concern. From a few passages on the subject, we gather it was mystical and practical (i.e., ethical); a lifting of the spirit to God, a converting of love into action: ' To dwell in Christ (*John* xv) means to adapt the doctrine and principles of Christ to a new condition and attitude . . . putting Christian doctrine into practice to the inward true welfare of men.' In the eighteenth century religion and ethics were so close to one another that it is possible Semler with his ' new condition ' and ' inner welfare ' meant a mystical pietistic new birth. In other passages he said that even unbaptized heathen who had heard the main points of Christian doctrine but had no opportunity for baptism, communion or Bible-reading, had part in ' spiritual religion ' and were possibly better Christians than the members of the outward Church communities; certainly here he was thinking of their human and moral qualities.

On the other hand, he once described mysticism as indispensable, ' as the surest stronghold of inner religion when it is both shut in and besieged by the tyrannical power of the outward Church.' In monasteries, cells and nunneries, he declared he had found so many true Christians it gave him strong confirmation of his belief that ' the infinite invisible city of God on earth ' was invincible and indestructible.

Not only the idea of Church but the idea of religion itself had grown inwards, and at the same time nebulous.

' The power of Christianity cannot be bound to the Greek or Latin or German Bible, and not to preacher nor to sacrament.' Other people might find these aids useful on occasion, and for the ' rude common masses ' they were so without doubt, to restrain them from vice. Eventually they only constituted the ABC of real Christianity. Mysticism in its highest flights entailed a spiritualization of Christianity that made it believe it could give up dogma and sacrament, and rationalism turned Christianity into a matter of practical living so that it actually did give up dogma and sacrament.

It is curious how the two movements intersected at an extreme point—in Semler. He had travelled along both paths. But by way of spiritual inner religion he reached the same goal almost effortlessly, and in one bound, to which, as rationalist theologian on the path of intelligible knowledge, he had advanced by slow, painful, arduous stages.

Gottfried Arnold as mystic and pietist had prepared the way for rationalism. Semler, the scholar of the enlightenment, showed how much room there was for the pietist legacy within rationalism. But there was one new element common to both, antagonistic to the old orthodox formality and destined to dominate spiritual life in Europe: this was *religious individualism*.

CHAPTER V

THE THEOLOGY OF REVELATION REVALUED: GOTTHOLD EPHRAIM LESSING

CHRISTIAN IDEAS WITH NO RELIGIOUS CONTENT

GOTTHOLD EPHRAIM LESSING (1729–1781) was born in a Lutheran parsonage in Kamenz in the Electorate of Saxony. In 1746, in Leipzig, where Johann Sebastian Bach, then over sixty years of age, was cantor at the School of St. Thomas, he began to study theology. But he soon changed his subject and turned to literature, criticism, poetry and drama. He lived in Berlin, editing a newspaper, then in Breslau through the Seven Years War, as secretary to General Tauentzien, and in Hamburg as playwright to the National Theatre; finally, as librarian to Duke Charles of Brunswick, in Wolfenbüttel. In 1781, he set out on a short visit to Brunswick, but he was already ill and died there on February 15 at the age of 52.

1. LUTHER'S SPIRIT VERSUS LUTHER'S CHURCH

In the 1770's, under the title *Fragments by an unnamed Author*, Lessing published some essays by Hermann Samuel Reimarus (1694–1768), a philosopher of the *Aufklärung*, a deist, that is to say an opponent of revelation. He thus became engaged in a war of ideas with the Bible Lutherans whose spokesman was Johann Melchior Goeze (1717–1786), a leading pastor in the city of Hambourg. In the course of this campaign the contrast between orthodox ideas and 'enlightened' deistic ideas became plain. Lessing, the protagonist of the deistic cause, was persuaded that he was acting as the true authentic son of Luther and tried to brand-mark the strict Lutheranism of the orthodox as a defection.

His letter breaking with Goeze in February–March 1778, runs as follows:

> I will not have you run me down as though I meant less well by the Lutheran Church than you do. For I am conscious of being a far better friend to it than the man who would

persuade us that his own delicacy of feeling towards his remunerative pastorate (or whatever it may be) is holy zeal for the things of God. Do you really suppose, Mr. Pastor, that you have the slightest spark of the Lutheran spirit? . . . Would that he could hear me, he whom I should prefer for my judge above all others: Thou, Luther, misunderstood great man! and by no one more than by the short-sighted, stubborn fellows who go with thy slippers in their hands, proclaiming the way thou didst strike out for them, but straying from it themselves. . . . Thou didst free us from the yoke of tradition: who will free us from the unendurable yoke of the letter! Who is going to bring us Christianity such as thou wouldest teach it to-day; such as Christ would teach it! Who . . .

Lessing upheld the idea of a true spiritual Lutheranism as opposed to the servile and too literal Lutheranism of the strictly orthodox. He accused Goeze of exaggerating orthodoxy, of remaining cold to the Lutheran spirit while preaching the letter of Lutheran doctrine. And then he indicated himself, the *aufklärer* on the brim of disbelief, as having a better understanding of the Church of Luther than the strict Lutherans;—calling upon the reformer to judge as between his cause and Goeze's.

Lessing believed—or made out that he believed—he was defending Luther's cause against the Lutheran Church. He could only make this appear credible by declaring individual independent religious experience as proclaimed by Semler to be a first principle of Luther's, and all that came in conflict with it, for instance the established teaching of the Lutheran Church, to be opposed to Luther.

The true Lutheran does not take refuge in Luther's writings but in Luther's spirit; and Luther's spirit makes the absolute demand that no man be prevented from going the way of his own discretion as prompted by his own experience of truth. But all are prevented if only one is forbidden to communicate his advances in experience. For without communication from one to another no total advance is possible.

In other words, there are degrees of perfection in the experience of truth arising out of the free play of thought in each individual case.

Progress was what Luther intended, but the Lutherans prohibited and suppressed it. Therefore the Lutherans were papists while Lessing and those of like mind to him were the lawful heirs.

> Mr. Pastor [he wrote in the first 'Anti-Goeze' in 1778], if you turn our Lutheran pastors into our popes, and they may prescribe where we must stop short in Scriptural research and sets limits to our research activities and to our publishing them, then I shall be the first to exchange the little popes for the real Pope.

2. LESSING AND LUTHER'S BIBLE

The occasion for open warfare was provided by a translation of the Bible by Karl Friedrich Bahrdt (1741–1792). He was one of the radical theologians of the enlightenment who was merciless to the traditional faith. 'Dr. Bahrdt snips away from the Church system everything that does not flatly accord with his ideas,' remarked Baron von Knigge in his contemporary novel *The Journey to Brunswick*.

During the years 1773–75, Bahrdt brought out a 'sample translation' of the New Testament that was actually banned by law for misrepresenting the Christian Gospel. The Lutherans were greatly disturbed by this translation, Lessing defended it. Goeze was quite within his rights when he drew attention to Bahrdt's distortion of the basic truths of Christianity and took steps to have the book banned. This action Lessing attacked:

> What a fine state of affairs, and so true to the spirit of Luther: A Lutherish pastor attempts to induce the Reich Council to take steps which, if they had seriously been taken 250 years ago, would have deprived us of the Reformation altogether. What rights did Luther have that do not belong to every doctor of theology to-day? If nowadays a doctor of theology is not to be allowed to translate the Bible anew, in

a way that he is ready to answer for before God and his conscience: no more was Luther to be allowed to do it. I will go
further: Luther even less. [For in Luther's time it was still a
debatable point whether it was or was not a good thing for the
ordinary man to read the Gospel in his mother tongue. But
for the Protestant of the eighteenth century, this is no longer
debatable but clear as daylight.]

In short, to condemn Bahrdt's or any other contemporary's
translation is to call Luther's translation to account, however
much the one may deviate from the other. Luther's translation
took the accepted translation of his time as its point of departure
too; whether more or less so is irrelevant.

It is impossible [said Lessing] for Mr. Goeze to speak more
harmfully of Bahrdt's translation than Emser did of Luther's.
I have not, however, the slightest intention of setting up as
the champion of Bahrdt's translation: I merely wish to support
his warrant to translate according to his conscience, for it is
certainly no whit less valid than Luther's warrant.

According to Goeze, Bahrdt's interpretation distorted the
meaning of the Bible, and that was why his version should be
put on the Index. Lessing was not going to let himself become
involved in the Christian aspect of the question, for him it was
purely a matter of rights. Luther was a doctor of theology.
Good, so was Bahrdt. Luther had permitted himself to translate
the Bible according to his conscience. If it was right for him to
do it, then it was right for Bahrdt too. Whether the content of
the Bahrdt interpretation deviated from the Lutheran or not was
irrelevant, in view of the fact that Luther's translation itself
deviated from those current in his day. Bahrdt could translate
Holy Scripture as he pleased: to translate was his right as a
Lutheran; and whoever would contest this right was guilty of
attacking a first principle of Luther's.

Thus Lessing developed the idea of a formal Lutheranism,
by which he understood the right of Protestants to freedom in
religious matters after Luther's example. You were not required
to have any object in view; that is, you did not have to conform

at all to Luther's doctrine. It was only important that every step taken should be according to conscience. In the chapters on pietism and on Semler, we saw how this conception of conscience undermined the very foundations of orthodox Lutheranism. In Lessing we see how he applied the principle to himself in *Nathan the Wise* and *The Education of the Human Race*, and, assuming that religious belief must have a content, reached the very verge of unbelief.

But the orthodox Lutherans were in the main current of a tradition a thousand years old, when they held Holy Scripture to be inspired as a whole, and venerated it as the work of the Holy Ghost. Leasing would have none of this.

Among his posthumous papers there was one entitled ' Bibliolatry,' directed against ' idolatry ' in regard to the Bible. Luther was not exempted. But although Luther more than once called the Holy Scriptures ' God,' or ' the spiritual body of Christ,' Lessing was prepared to overlook it because he was, apart from this, a great man who had the courage to discard opinions or change them for the better. The Protestants who followed Luther were, however, literally inexcusable, and the whole of the Christian past was called to account for ' multifarious superstition ' (' the Gospel being particularly exposed to this during the Dark Ages '), and also for its ' servile attitude to the mere book, almost wholly neglecting its spirit.'

Lessing who had said, ' the true Lutheran will not seek refuge in Luther's writings but in Luther's spirit,' now proclaimed, in equally forthright tones, the letter is not the spirit and the Bible is not the whole of religion. But within the Bible he distinguished between Holy Writ (taken as a whole) and a (special) word of God. He produced very ingenious arguments in support of this theory. The Bible, he said, contains a good deal that is not purely religious. Taken as a whole it is but a book, literal. Its religious content must be extracted. The extracted is the ' better part ' of the Bible, its spirit, and can only be the books and passages ' more or less directly concerned with our improvement.' In order to give force to his views he added: ' In my opinion it verges on blasphemy to suppose the Holy Ghost would display his power equally effectively in the genealogical tables of Esau's posterity in the Book of Moses, and the Sermon on the Mount of Jesus in Matthew.' And he closed the argument by stating that the distinction between spirit and letter was held by other ' no less good Lutheran theologians,' and he was only treading in their footsteps.

In actual fact, he was throwing all doors open to arbitrariness in religious thought. Who was to decide what passages were conducive to spiritual improvement? Simply, each individual for himself, for Churches and pastors were not to be recognized as authorities. In practice it worked out like this: every man picked out the passages that appealed to him, and what did not appeal to him he discarded as ' literal ' and non-religious. With no objective norm, and no authority available, it was extremely likely that the variety of points of view would produce an equal variety of interpretations.

The strict Lutherans taught, as Luther did, that the only source of Christian belief was the Bible, and it contained the whole Christian religion. Pastor Goeze considered it to be his duty, as a leading Lutheran, to intervene when Lessing published the anti-Christian *Fragments*. He decried him publicly as an enemy of the faith and of Christianity. But Lessing was determined to win, and to do so by convincing public opinion that Goeze's Lutheranism and Christianity were far from impeccable, and that he, Lessing, was the true defender of Christianity. He set to work skilfully, but he would probably have been wiser to desist. It was not quite above board for the author of *Nathan* to fall back upon a Catholic doctrine—that the authority of the Bible is subject to the Church—in order to undermine the authority of Holy Scripture in Protestant minds.

3. RELIGION CEASES TO BE CHRISTIAN

A gap now appeared between the religious opinions Lessing gave out as his and his real personal point of view. He was determined to win the fight with Goeze and posed as the true Lutheran, the advocate of Christianity.

For example, Goeze stated that all Christians, regardless of confessional differences, ' held the Bible to be the only source of Christian doctrine' (for the reformed Churches, of course), ' without which it could neither be proved nor propagated, nor in fact exist.' Lessing rightly contested this: for Catholics the Church is the source of doctrine, the Scriptures are subordinate, and in addition to Scripture, tradition must be taken into account. Otherwise one would have to suppose (he said) ' that any reasonable man, even if he knew nothing of Christianity at all, could entirely alone discover the whole of Christianity in the New Testament books and disentangle it by himself; I doubt it very much.'[1] As a statement it is unimpeachable. But it was made defensively and was lacking in detachment. This man Goeze is threatening me, he complained: a Lutheran pastor and a rotten advocate is threatening me with the public prosecutor, and on no other grounds than that I am a man

> who is forthright enough to prefer, as a Lutheran, to take refuge in a doctrine of the Roman Church rather than let the whole Christian religion succumb to the objections of the freethinkers: these objections refer simply to the Bible; not to religion, to the book alone; it is true, the strict Lutherans have a newfangled and still unproved doctrine that religion is only to be found in the Book.

Goeze insisted that there could be no Christian religion at all if the Bible were not entirely what the Lutheran (alone) holds it to be, and this Lessing declared to be ' un-Christian' in one of the ' Letters to Dr. Walch,' advancing the incisive counter-claim that Pastor Goeze maintained this opinion ' defiantly and ignorantly . . . to the patent disadvantage of Christianity as a whole, in order to score an illusory point for his own party.' To his patron, Charles I, Duke of Brunswick (1735–1780), he depicted

---

[1] This line of thought, developed in conjunction with his study of the Church Fathers, brought him to the hypothesis of the possible existence of one original Christian document, the source alike of tradition, the Nicene creed and the canonicity of the Bible in its present form; in 1780 he discussed the idea in the ' Letter to Dr. Walch.'

Goeze as a man 'intolerant of the most harmless opinions' if they did not coincide with his own, the Hambourg pastor only warming to the debate for the sake of airing his own views, not for religion. Two-thirds of all Lutheran divines, he said, had affirmed their desire to have nothing to do with Goeze's type of religion. In the same letter, Lessing described himself as the man who, as 'all Germany' would testify, had 'proved himself on all occasions to be a most orthodox defender of Lutheran doctrine.'

The *Reimarus Fragments* could certainly not be taken as an apology for Christianity, for their publication signified an advance into the limelight of a deism that rejected revelation. A Christian Lutheran with a sense of responsibility towards his religion was bound to protest. And a Lutheran dignitary such as the Duke of Brunswick saw himself obliged to forbid the further publication of fragments of this sort, when the Consistorium required it. Lessing sought to have the ban repealed after it was issued, out of regard for his own would-be blameless Lutheranism. He let it be understood that the opinions in the *Fragments* were not necessarily his own, and begged his lord the duke to note that it was customary to let unbelievers make known their objections to religion, in order to afford occasion for the faithful to answer back; not to leave our faith open to the accusation that it 'suppressed all opposition.' Further he said that he had, 'though superfluously,' himself 'immediately provided the said *Fragments* with a refutation, which had gained the approval of the most unimpeachable Lutheran theologians, and in part won such high praise that modesty prevents my repeating it.'

In actual fact, Lessing's campaign was directed against Lutherans who believed in revelation. His intention seems to have been to propagate a theistic, undogmatic religion of humanity. But this came to light only in his last works, *Nathan* and *The Education of the Human Race*. Up to that point, one is tempted to say he fought in the disguise of a Lutheran and patron of Christianity, of a tolerant Christian rising above confessional differences. Practically, his aim was to get rid of Lutheran opposition, and all means were good means to wipe it out of existence. When the *Corpus Evangelicorum* of the German Reichstag and the High Court were invited to take up the Lutheran defence, Lessing wrote to his brother how he planned to conduct his case:

> I do not think I have much to fear from either. I have a safe method for splitting the High Court and setting it at sixes and sevens with itself, like Paul and the Sanhedrin. Namely, most members of it being Catholic, I have only to present my case in a particular way, and the condemnation which the Lutherans will pronounce will actually involve the condemnation of all the papists too, for they no more accept religion founded on Scripture and Scripture alone than I do. With this in mind, I have already written a page or two which I will enclose. You will see that I have adopted a line which should cause the eminent pastor to capitulate.

Many other passages show how Lessing's Lutheranism and Christianity were only such in name (and finally not even that): their content was not Christian.

Before he died, he made the attempt to give his ideas on religion artistic form in *Nathan* and historical and philosophic form in *The Education of the Human Race*. But hints of his real attitude occur as early as the *Refutations*, or better *Commentaries*, to the *Reimarus Fragments*, and can be traced back to a paper entitled *Thoughts on the Herrnhuter* written in his twenty-first year (1750). In this early work he set down his ideas on the state of religion at the expiry of biblical and Christian history—a medley of current Protestant notions (ranging from the ' darkness ' of the late classical and mediæval centuries to the ' wicked coercive institution ' of the papacy) spiced with pietistic ethics and ' enlightened ' reason.

He describes history in terms of ' high moments ' and we see in what light the third high moment, the Reformation, appeared to Lessing as a young man—at the time of Goethe's birth. He saw it as the work of men and a movement towards freedom of the understanding, as opposed to superstition. ' They are well known, the men who in those unworthy days first attempted to see with their own eyes again. Human understanding may submit to a yoke, but if it is too heavy it will be shaken off.' The intention of the Reformation was the reinstitution of religion in its purity.

What a cruel fate it was [said Lessing ruefully] that let two men differ over words, a mere trifle [the dogma of the Lord's Supper], when they could so much more usefully have set about reinstating religion in its former splendour, had they but joined forces. Blessed men . . . who steadied the trembling crowns on the heads of kings. . . . But how was it that virtue and holiness gained so little from your improvements?

The answer is contained in his next question and shows why a decline followed the third high moment: ' Of what good is right belief in a wrong light? Would you had left us as many pious followers as you did learned ones!' Superstition, Lessing declared, was done for; but reason and knowledge which brought men to truth led them away from 'the practice of the duties of a Christian.' He rounded off his paragraph with the remark: ' In knowing we are angels and in living devils.' It has a very pietistic ring.

Lessing admitted that the Reformation issued from a common Evangelical tradition as did Semler and other Evangelical thinkers of the enlightenment. But it was accepted not because it introduced pure Christian doctrine (orthodoxy), not exclusively because it had introduced freedom of conscience (pietism; Semler), but because with the Reformation the age of clear reason began and the age of dark superstition was over. The strict believers of the seventeenth century and the eighteenth-century enlightenment all looked upon Luther symbolically as the bringer of light. In the seventeenth century not a few coins were struck portraying Luther holding high a burning torch which he had snatched from under a bushel.

By light the orthodox meant doctrine, the *Aufklärung* the light of human understanding, which freed men from the chains of superstition and doctrinal intransigeance, and was of itself sufficient to put them in possession of the perceptible world.

To Lessing's way of thinking, the main deficiency of the men who continued the Reformation was that their claim to hold the true doctrine was not offset by holiness of living. Few witnesses show so clearly how effectively pietism assisted at the birth of the *Aufklärung*.

Even in this early work, Lessing is not far from identifying religion with virtue. The distinguishing mark of the first Christians was, in his view, their virtuousness and their 'holy way of life.' And the weakness of the Christians of the reformed faith was a lack of virtue, holiness and right living. The mediæval Church declined because contemplation was preferred to 'practical Christianity.' As to the person of Christ, Lessing makes no mention of the command that we must believe in him in order to gain salvation—of the fact that we owe our redemption to him; but says rather: 'I must confess I regard him merely as a divinely inspired teacher,' and again, that he had 'motives' which claimed to be religious in order to achieve certain effects. Namely, 'to revive religion in its full purity, and to set it within those bounds where its effects are the more wholesome, the straiter the bounds are laid.' And in this he included the 'spiritualization of God.' 'God is a spirit, you should worship him in spirit. On this more than all else did Christ insist. And what text is more apt to bind all kinds of religion to one another?' At root this was a rejection of the 'Lord God' of the Old Testament, the 'Father' of the New, in the name of an all-embracing tolerance. For God in the Bible does indeed desire all men and all nations to attain to salvation through Christ, but forbids the worship of any other gods whatsoever, under pain of terrible punishment.

The second *Reimarus Fragment* treated of the 'impossibility of a revelation in which all men should believe along certain set lines.' Every man, be he ever so great a scholar, Reimarus continued—a Grotius, a Bellarmine, or whoever he may be—discovers in the Scripture only what his Lutheran, or Armenian, or Tridentine child's catechism taught him. He goes to the Bible with his mind made up. 'For the great majority of people, not excluding men of learning, it is impossible to build a true

EPHRAIM LESSING

FREDERICK
THE GREAT

JUSTUS
MÖSER

system of belief out of their own reading of the Scriptures. There is nothing left but for each to abide by the creed he was taught in childhood, which is simply follow-my-leader into prejudice, darkness, and mirage, certainly no securely grounded faith.' The faith of a Christian bound to his particular confession is no proper Christian faith but blind dependence on formulæ learnt by heart, of highly dubious trustworthiness. It was at this point in the argument that Lessing cleverly interposed his annotation to the second *Fragment*:

> This is the place to call our author to task, once and for all, though what I say may be read as excuse as much as blame. He takes the sole really true form of Christianity to be all that is included in a certain system set out in certain symbolical books—whether it be from passages essential to Christianity, seeing it was taught in those express terms by its founder, or passages that are there merely to establish a certain sequence of events—it is all the same to him. . . .

Once more the separation of religion and dogma is formulated as sharply as possible. In other words, Christian doctrine and Christianity proper are two different things.

'Religion,' remarked Lessing, 'is not true because the evangelists and apostles taught it, but they taught it because it is true. The traditional Scriptures are only to be explained by their inner truth, and no Scripture can give religion an inner truth if it has none of its own.

This is a plain denial of the objectivity of the Christian religion. For the 'inner truth' was only there for the man who felt it, what was felt could be entirely different for each different individual, so that in the long run, the interpretation, the good repute, and the validity, of the Christian revelation were matters dependent on subjective, individual picking and choosing. Thus the intrinsic nature of revelation, as coming from without and from above, was implicitly rejected.

In the summer of 1780, as Friedrich Heinrich Jacobi reports, Lessing admitted in a conversation: 'The orthodox conceptions of godhead are no longer mine, I cannot accept them.

Ev χαὶ πᾶυ! That is all I know.—As a term of reference, if one is required of me, I can only name Spinoza.'

So Christianity, and even deism, were cast aside, in favour of pantheism.

From an historical point of view, this step was the inevitable outcome of a development which started with the rejection of the Church as objective reality, went on to the rejection of a formulated creed, and led to tolerance; furthermore, it went from the shrinking of personal religion to 'inner light,' to a more and more exclusive reduction of religion to reason and feeling.[1]

This meant the identifying of God with nature (in its Christian sense) and constituted belief in a *natural* (as opposed to a *revealed*) religion.

It was already clear to those of Lessing's contemporaries who were aware of the implications of their faith, that his standpoint was not to be reconciled with Christian thought.[2]

From the Christian point of view, the question of who best defended the bastions of the faith—Lessing or Goeze—must take into account the forking of the roads when, with Lessing, German thought rejected Christianity.

We know Herder's seductively lovely hailing of Lessing as ' seeker of the truth, knower of the truth, defender of the truth ' —as the man who preferred the search for truth to the possession of it, as the relentless foe of hypocrisy. But we should not

---

[1] In Western European thought this development became paramount and irresistible by 1700, but remained in sharp opposition to Catholic theology and could never on any account fall back on it—unlike the German *Aufklärung*, which boasted of its descent from the Reformation idea of conscience.

[2] It is possible to enquire with Karl Barth (*Protestant Theology in the Nineteenth Century. Its pre-history and its history.* Zollikon/Zürich. 1948, § 6: Lessing, pp. 235 *sqq.*) whether Lessing did not read into the old word ' revelation ' an entirely new meaning, through an identification of the Christian lord of history (as in *The Education of the Human Race*) with a humanity in process of developing or of educating itself. O. Mann says (*Lessing, Sein und Leistung*, 1948) that a time may come when the Bible will lose its absolute religious validity, through the fact that a man arrives at what it teaches ' by way of reason and action,' and ' the Gospels as goal for the future ' become ' redundant.'

overlook the manly and Christian stand of the much-abused
Goeze confronting his lively opponent Lessing:

Dear Mr. Councillor [he wrote in the thick of battle],
please do not be angry if on this occasion I speak to you in a
tone entirely different from the one you have wrung from me
hitherto. God knows, I love you dearly. Nor do I underrate
the admirable talents which the goodness of God has bestowed
on you, nor the superior knowledge and perceptions you have
acquired by the right use of those talents in various branches
of the so-called Arts. I forgive you whole-heartedly for
applying all your powers to ruining me in the eyes of the
Church, of the world of learning, and of my parishioners. . . .
But it is this very love and regard for you which moves me to
entreat you, before the face of God, to ponder deeply what I
have to say, in some quiet hour, when your passions are not
seething. You declare—and my whole heart trembles at this
declaration—that you will not shudder at the hour of your
death on account of the printing of this *Fragment* and what
was thereby done. For God's sake, and for the sake of your
eternal salvation, reflect upon what you wrote. Ah, do not
shut yourself off from the way of repentance in this manner,
the time may come when you will not find that way again
and may never be in that state when you would seek it in
tears. Think of the account the Lord will require of you on
that Day for what you then did—the Lord whose Honour is
so wantonly attacked and slandered by the *Fragments*, whose
Word you seek to place so low beneath mere miserable human
authorship. Enquire of your conscience whether it has a lively
assurance that the mock-reasons you give to justify it—though
they may dazzle the eyes of weak Christians, and still more of
free-thinkers—can have any worth for Him whose Eyes are
brighter than flames of fire? Imagine that on that Day not one
but hundreds will stand out against you saying: ' Lord! We
died in unbelief, but either we did formerly believe in thee, or
we would later have come to believe, for our hearts were not
yet wholly blocked and there were times when thy Word

caused us to be deeply moved. That man alone is cause that we then stubbornly opposed thy Spirit. . . . Lord, be thou Judge between him and us!'

Johann Georg Hamann, the Magus of the North, testifies how he recognized in Lessing 'a great figure in our literary world,' having 'come to know him personally in Hambourg as very friendly, manly and honourable.' Three years after Lessing's death, on December 5, 1784, in a letter to Friedrich Heinrich Jacobi, after paying all honour due to Lessing's intellectual achievement, he considered what even to-day a Christian had to take into account:

In what concerns Lessing, . . . frankly, my excellent friend, what do you make of the man's honesty and sincerity in the whole business of the *Fragments*? However dull-witted, was not the Hambourger Goeze fundamentally right? When one's head is full of pantheistic ideas, is it actually possible to say a Christian ' Our Father '?

CHAPTER VI

THE POLITICAL FIELD:
FREDERICK THE GREAT—JUSTUS MÖSER

1. FREDERICK THE GREAT

FREDERICK THE GREAT and Justus Möser were not men to indulge in theological speculation. They had pronounced practical interests which claimed their attention, and were in this respect a contrast to Lessing with his tendency to direct reflection on worldly affairs on to theological lines. But both found occasion to express views on Luther and the Reformation. These men are of interest, not so much as Lutherans, but as key-minds of the century. But we may well wonder whether there is any vital difference between the views of the theologians of the time and those of other German *aufklärer* unburdened with Protestant preoccupations.

Crown Prince Frederick, as a young man of 25, wrote to Voltaire on May 14, 1737:

> Incontestably [the northern rulers] have much to thank Luther and Calvin for (poor devils in any case): they freed them from the yoke of the priesthood and considerably increased their incomes by the addition of church property; nonetheless their religion still remains impure with superstition and bigotry.

The man was ridiculed, the political gain warmly commended, and to this extent the Reformation was approved of, though an 'enlightened' ruler could find little of interest in the spiritual and religious side of it.

We observe the patronizing tone. There is more to it than the manner natural to his position, he really regretted that Luther did not risk going further.

> If I had lived in Martin Luther's time I should have supported him wholeheartedly, and encouraged him to push on

to Socinianism, which really is a one-God religion. But that monk and his company raised the curtain just so far and no further, and bequeathed for enlightenment many a dark spot.

As a cultured, reasonable European of the eighteenth century, he enjoyed a sense of superiority over the crude sixteenth century:

If one merely considers the gross coarseness of his style, Martin Luther is nothing but a blustering monk and a crude writer for somewhat unenlightened people. But before blaming him, however rightly, for his eternal insults and invective, one must remember that those he was writing for could only be touched by curses and were not accessible to arguments.

Frederick the ruler enquired what Luther's Reformation had done for the State; Frederick the philosopher wanted to know what it had contributed to the progress and enlightenment of humanity.

(a) THE REFORMATION AND POLITICS

The wars of religion which swept over Europe in the sixteenth and seventeenth centuries counted among the evils the Reformation had wrought. The king sought the deeper cause in the confusion and disorder created by the ecclesiastical changes, but the immediate cause was the ' hatred of the priests ' who interfered with the policies of the rulers. Otherwise, himself a ruler, he was pleased with what the Reformation had done. It was a commonplace of the *Aufklärung* that in the Middle Ages the popes by means of the ubiquitous hierarchy had ruled the nations, not by right but none the less in fact. Princes and subjects alike were reduced to servitude. Frederick had no reason for not sharing these views. ('The priests took away the people's goods and freedom.') But he was open-minded enough to appreciate the dazzling prospects that Luther's preaching opened out for the regional princes, and the political advantage was quite sufficient motivation for a change of faith. 'He was soon leader of the movement, and as his doctrine questioned the rights of bishops to benefices and monasteries to property, the princes flocked to the reformer.' The king was thirty-five, had just won the second Silesian war and was writing the *Memoirs of the House of Brandenburg*. The Foreword to Fleury's Church History written a year after the end of the Seven Years War contains the following: ' If Luther had done no more than free the princes and peoples from the servitude in which Roman rule held them shackled, he would still deserve to have altars raised to him as the liberator of his country.' The greatest benefit was the transfer of the high episcopacy, the highest ecclesiastical superintendence, to the regional rulers.

Now of its nature the Church is a structure that strikes root independently and has its own rights over and against the State; of divine origin (founded on Word and Sacrament) and with divine right. Therefore independent of the State; but bound to it not least by the fact that the people who belong to it as members serve the State as citizens. A coming to terms of the two orders, State and Church, is wholly unavoidable so long as both exist. But the circumstances of their relationship are fluctuating and variable. When the Reformation in Protestant lands decided that the Protestant civic authorities should hold the highest pastoral office and have the last word in Church affairs in their regions, from the ecclesiastical point of view it was at the cost of the independence essential to the very nature of a Church. The original Church, the old and mediæval Church, and the Catholic Church of modern times in the lands remaining to it, had safeguarded this independence by the institution of the papacy. Focused as it is on an other-worldly reality, the Church must see subordination to the State in spiritual matters, even were the authority concerned Christian, as an act of self-immolation contrary to its nature. The *Aufklärung*, with its this-worldly focus on matters of State, reason, morals and humanity, found it an admirable arrangement, for it gave the State high religious-worldly prestige; State-consciousness had become so sensitive that it reacted automatically to every intrusion in the political sphere. The dependence of the regional churches was now taken for granted and even to think of their independence was a disturbance to public order and a threat to the State.

Dilating on the varieties of religions, Frederick granted that from a purely political standpoint the Protestant religion seemed to be the most bearable.

> In a monarchy, the Protestant religion, which depends on no one, is completely subject to the government. But Catholicism establishes in the heart of the secular State an all-powerful spiritual State full of tricks and intrigues. The priests who rule consciences and have no superior other than the Pope, are more masters of the people than their rightful rulers. . . .

Also, ' in a State that . . . needs subjects, citizens who make vows to let the human race die out must be a real danger.'

At bottom, the king had no notion that freedom was of the very nature of the Church; nor that a Christian renunciation of marriage was a way of following our Lord, who told us not to love wife, brother and parents more than himself. Neither freedom nor celibacy was however in favour in Protestantism. The latter was turned down by Luther, and true independence had *de facto* been handed over to the State. Rightly understood, it was its un-Catholic side that Frederick valued in Protestantism. But that was not its strongest side from a Christian point of view; given the circumstances, it could even become a Christian no-man's land.

(b) THE REFORMATION IN THE LIGHT OF THE ' AUFKLÄRUNG '

It was Frederick's habit to adorn his political considerations with marginal observations. His sceptical view of humanity affected his outlook on history. He traced the Reformation to motives of self-seeking and ambition. A revolution in religious standpoint was incapable, he held, of producing a renewal of the Church, for ' few people engage in abstract ideas, and the number of those who think deeply about such weighty matters is still smaller.' So it was not the violation of consciences by the clergy that started the Reformation off, but the cause lay rather in the reduction to material servitude of the nations and their citizens. *Rebus sic stantibus*, Frederick said the Reformation was inevitable in any case, even if the clergy had not let it loose by internal discord in the indulgence controversy between Augustinians and Dominicans. The Augustinians declared against the Pope; Luther, ' a Saxon monk of daredevil boldness, with a powerful imagination, cunning enough to exploit the fermentation of ideas, became the head of the party that declared war on Rome '; he attacked the abuses and with a bold hand swept away ' the bonds of superstition.'

There we have the key-words: the Reformation meant purifying the Church of abuse and superstition. Of the two, superstition was if anything the worse. If an *aufklärer* spoke of the salutary results of the Reformation, he usually meant the overcoming of error and superstition, the dawn of the rule of reason. Thus Frederick called the Reformation ' a blessing for the world and in general for the progress of the human mind.' Reason, tolerance, virtue, science have henceforth replaced ignorance, intolerance, and unreason. As the Protestants now had to reflect on matters of faith, ' they set aside at a stroke all prejudices of education, and learnt to make free use of their reason; reason which is given to men for their guidance, to be followed at least on the more important occasions of their life.' Human reason was capable of development, but ' only in the holy havens of tolerance set up by the Protestant states.' The king thought the Protestant reformers were tolerant because they were persecuted; but here he was greatly mistaken.

With satisfaction he observed that competition between the Churches spurred the theologians on to higher achievement: in order to be in a position to defend their side in controversy, they had to get down to their studies. Thus ignorance disappeared from the professorial chairs. Equally advantageous for outward effect was the multiplicity of confessions, for the Catholic and Protestant clergy looked one another up and down with a critical eye, and were thus obliged to behave themselves. Once in a single short phrase he named the ' incalculable benefit ' that accrued from the Reformation: freedom of thought. But it all had to be weighed in the balance with evils of such heavy import that in the king's opinion the gain was dearly paid for.

He was thinking of the hundred-year wars of religion. Like everyone else under the spell of the notion of progress, Frederick saw history as growth and development. Starting primitively, striving purposefully to reach a condition as near perfection as possible, the generations and races had their shoulder to the wheel. For the *Aufklärung*, the favourite symbol was the rising sun scattering with its rays the vestigial darkness of bygone days. But when Frederick examined the Reformation, he found it wanting.

> The Reformation could not destroy all errors. It is true it opened people's eyes to a number of superstitions, but it still safeguarded a number of others. So ineradicable is man's inclination to error. Though Luther did not believe in purgatory, he kept ghosts and devils in his doctrine. He even claimed that Satan appeared to him in Wittenberg and that he drove him away by throwing an ink-pot at his head. There was hardly a nation at that time that was not full of notions of that sort.

Nonetheless, if the Reformation was backward compared with what was to follow, in its own time it was an immense step forward. As to the 1200 years between the Council of Nicea and the posting of the theses in Wittenberg, all that the king had to say was this: ' I incline to the assumption that the whole world from Constantine to Luther was weak-minded.'

(c) HISTORICAL VIEW OF CHRISTIANITY

The thousand years when the king considered the whole world to be of unsound mind were precisely those dedicated to the immense task of establishing the world in an other-worldly order. The king did not know and did not understand. When in the last years of the Seven Years War he read Abbé Fleury's Church History, it was not with a view to a better understanding: ' A consequential history of religion . . . makes instructive reading for anyone who reflects on the human mind.' In a letter to his friend, the Duchess Luise Dorothea of Gotha, he made comments on religion of which no orthodox Lutheran pastor could have approved, and added himself that he would never have been accepted as orthodox by the former strict Gotha Superintendent and his consistorium. But it did not worry him.

I had rather appear right-thinking before reason, which is given to man to find his way through life, than before a gathering of Church doctors basing their statements on Esra, Matthew, John, Paul and the whole crowd of apostles of superstition who deluded and stultified the world.

He could not help noticing that Christianity had a certain greatness of its own in the past, but the *Aufklärung*, with its notion of a religion founded exclusively on natural perception and reason, had no use for a gospel of redemption through God made Man. Nor had Frederick.

He traced the early expansion of Christianity to conditions reigning at the time within the Roman Empire and to the ethical character of the new religion.

The Christian religion began to expand at the time when the Roman Empire suffered under the tyranny of blood-thirsty villains who ruled it successively. The ordinary citizen, who under their bloody rule was prepared for anything that can befall a man, found consolation and approbation in his great suffering nowhere but in stoicism. The Christian ethic was related to stoical doctrine: that is what accounts for the rapid progress Christianity made.

The Church was the means by which violent or cunning ecclesiastical ambition rose to power. Originally the Church was constituted a republic. Since Constantine a sort of aristocracy had formed, the popes, emperors and distinguished elders then playing leading parts.

As time went on, this form of government experienced change, as all things human do. When ambitious men coquet together for power and consideration, they spare neither cunning nor craft to usurp another's place and the final victory goes to the slyest. This time the most cunning were the popes:

they used the weaknesses of the Eastern Roman Empire to seize upon the Cæsars' power and transfer the rights of the imperial crown to the papal tiara.

The authority which the Church hierarchy enjoyed among Christians could be traced to its undertakings in the creative line: ' As founders of new dogma the bishops must necessarily have been conscious of their power and influence. It lies in human nature to utilize to the full the advantages one has.'

The creeds and articles of faith formulated by the old Church were the creation of the Church rulers. At best the work of the human intellect, more likely a production of power politics with a view to domination. In the first three hundred years the Church was praiseworthy in that the clergy were without power or means to impose their way of thinking on their opponents, but it was regrettable that under Constantine all that changed:

He was hardly set on the throne when he prescribed an œcumenical council at Nicea (325). Of the Church Fathers who appeared at this council, three hundred voted against Arius. They roundly declared and confirmed that Christ was God, included in their creed the words ' only-begotten Son of God ' and excommunicated the Arians. Thus new dogma grew out of every church assembly. By the Council of Constantinople (381) it was the turn of the Holy Spirit.

If the creeds are mere creations of the bishops, it is no longer so certain that the faith proclaimed by the Church can be traced back to Christ, and there is not much left of the preaching of the Gospel by Christ and the Apostles. This was quite clear to Frederick. Christianity had begun modestly ' like all other worldly powers.'

The hero of this sect is a Jew from the dregs of the people, of doubtful origin, who wove a good moral teaching into the insipidities of old Hebraic lore, to whom miracles are ascribed, and who was finally condemned to an ignominious death. Twelve fanatics spread his teaching from the East to Italy; they won assent owing to their pure and holy moral life.

They preached, and what they taught—apart from a few miracles which might excite people with strong powers of self-delusion—was nothing but deism.

Rationally of course Frederick could not account for the principal facts of the Christian religion—incarnation, redemption and perfectibility. But his confidence in human reason was so entire that anything impervious to pure reason was discarded as fanaticism and superstition.

> Who, running through Church history, could not perceive that it is all of human making? What a miserable part God is allotted! He sends his only son into the world. This son is God. He sacrifices himself to reconcile his creation. He becomes man to improve the human race. What is the outcome of this great sacrifice? The world remains as corrupt as it was before his coming. The God who said: 'Let there be light!'—and there was light—would use such insufficient means to attain his worshipful ends? One single act of will were enough to ban spiritual and physical evil from the world, inspire the peoples with whatever faith he chose, and make them happy in the ways that lie open to his Almightiness. Only limited and narrow minds dare to ascribe to God a line of conduct so unworthy of his Worshipful Providence, letting him, through one of the greatest miracles, undertake a work doomed to failure.

(d) THE RELATIVE ADVANTAGES OF PROTESTANTISM— TOLERANCE AND RESIGNATION

The king had lost his faith. But he had views on Protestantism. At the age of seventy he told his brother Henry: 'If I had the choice between all Christian sects, I should declare for Protestantism because it does least harm.' At fifty he said the same in a letter to his friend the Duchess of Gotha. 'If one considers the religions as a philosopher, they are all much alike. Nonetheless the faith that is least infected with superstition deserves preference. That is without doubt Protestantism. It distinguishes itself too in not being bent on persecution. Those are the points that make me always declare for the faith of my fathers.' He liked Protestantism because it left him alone. Such a Protestantism existed only in his days, Calvin and Luther would not have pleased him at all.

He identified with Protestantism the idea of tolerance and religious freedom. The latter particularly is no genuinely Christian idea and given the circumstances can lead straight as a die out of the Christian field. ' I am firmly convinced,' said the king, ' that one must let everyone have the freedom to believe what he sees fit. If people want to believe in immortality I have nothing against it, provided that they do not persecute one another on that account.' This, in a letter to his brother Henry, points to the logical conclusion of the position taken up by Semler and Lessing in the name of Luther. ' If one keeps one's head and one's temper in a work of pure metaphysics,' he wrote to the Duchess of Gotha, ' . . . one can bear with the different beliefs of humanity, just as one puts up with the different physiognomies, clothes and habits which have become customary through long use.'

A substitution of values: *humanity* and *reason* replace the Christian values.

Although trusting reason implicitly and rejecting all truths that could not stand up to its scrutiny, he suffered from a deep sense of resignation, inclining to the view that truth remains inaccessible to mankind. He knew that truth is a main concern of religion, but truth was nonetheless only to be attained through ' enlightenment,' that is, through reason cleansed of prejudice and superstition and not through faith. ' I have much the same views on religions as Fontenelle, who said, if he had his hands full of truths he would not open them to release them to the people, for the people does not merit enlightenment.' But he was not really excluding himself when he wrote: ' Truth does not seem proper to man; his inheritance is error.'

The longer one lives in this world, the more does it appear that truth is not proper to all men. The veils of nature, the narrow confines of our own minds, the inclination to the

miraculous, of which everyone has his little share, self-seeking
and deceit which utilize the most crazy errors in order to win
consideration—in short everything points to the fact that we
live in a realm of delusion, and that apart from a few mathe-
matical truths it is not given us to attain to truth. All in all it
looks as though we are put into this world more to enjoy it
than to get to know it.

The king saw farther and more clearly than most and turned
his back on the reigning optimism of his age. Few men of the
enlightenment were convinced as he was of the frailty of human
existence. ' And well considered, what is life? ' On August 10,
1786, the king put the question to his sister Charlotte of
Brunswick, and answered it himself: ' It consists in seeing
one's fellow-citizens dying and coming into the world.'

A change had taken place in the course of his century, his
generation had lost touch with pietism, and he himself with the
native piety of his father. He knew human frailty through the
eyes of human perception, not the eyes of faith, and to such
awareness resignation, not hope, was the answer.

Otherwise his attitude was typical of his time. His tolerance
became proverbial; though he had a low opinion of mankind,
the idea of humanity was strong. In holding religions to be alike,
none sole possessor of the truth, he had the presentiment that
knowledge of truth is relative—not without that slight shudder
of prescience which always comes where faith has faltered. It is
all intimately connected with the search for a ' natural ' foundation for religion due to the ' impossibility ' of a supernatural
revealed religion. On this point King Frederick was completely
at one with the movement directed against the Christian revelation for which Reimarus and Lessing were responsible.

2. JUSTUS MÖSER

Legal adviser and historian to the high bishopric of Osnabrück, Justus Möser (1720–94) was, like Frederick, Lessing and
Semler, wholly a man of his time. His *Osnabrück History* (1768)
and his *Patriotic Phantasies* (1774–78) are known to historians.

In literature he owes his fame not least to the appreciation Goethe accorded him in Book III of *Wahrheit und Dichtung*. He specialized in German mediæval legal and constitutional history, and discovered the fundamental connexion between landed property, freedom and political order.

It distressed him when Voltaire, in his ' Letter on the English,' wrote disparagingly of the Reformation and put Luther, as well as Zwingli and Calvin, in the same rank as ' the ignorant' Mohammed. He felt called upon to correct this impression in an open letter intended for French consumption. The ' Letter ' must have been very widely read. Ten years later, Johann Georg Hamann, an East Prussian, wrote to his brother (1760):

> I send you a letter on Luther which I have come across here, from a certain Möser, who wrote a tragedy ' Arminius ' and is *advocatus patriæ* at the Osnabrück high bishopric. His style must be better in French than in German. Of his tragedy I have little good to say, it contains a very far-fetched witticism and a number of new German words. But his letter on Luther is excellent and I read it with uncommon pleasure, finding a heap of my own thoughts in it.

The letter is an apology for Luther by one of the most gifted men of the enlightenment, written with the intention of persuading one of the princes of the enlightenment (the world had produced no finer genius than Voltaire, said Frederick the Great) to a better understanding of Luther. It is significant that the author felt the rehabilitation to be complete the moment he had shown that Luther could survive eighteenth-century scrutiny unscathed. He drew a largely-conceived picture of Luther's character and pointed to his authorship as fit to entitle him to a place in the modern enlightened world.

(a) AN EIGHTEENTH-CENTURY LUTHER

He compared Luther to a commander-in-chief in genius, to a statesman, to a physician. The whole Reformation was displayed as a cleverly-planned campaign to overthrow the wrongful lordship of the Church and introduce a more ethical and orderly

JOHANN
GOTTFRIED HERDER

JOHANN
GEORG HAMANN

JOHANN WOLFGANG GOETHE

state of society. There were insurmountable difficulties to overcome: time-honoured prejudices; the power of custom; the
hatred, envy, enmity of hierarchies, princes and theologians.
Luther's undertakings testified to his ability 'to seize all
advantages, not missing a single one.'—'When he had once
made up his mind to reform the abuses, . . . he remained
steadfast and made such skilled use of his adversaries' faults that
one may say, if his spirit had inhabited the body of a general, he
would have been the greatest commander of his century.' It was
as 'the most skilful man' who 'knew how to recognize great
opportunities and seize them' that Luther had claim on the
consideration of posterity.

After his energy in action Möser admired Luther's exemplary
conduct; he did not teach 'merely like a sign-post' but went
ahead as a living example. 'He was no man to do things by
halves, and beat down all difficulties without heeding over-
discreet and fearful friends.' The Osnabrück *advocatus patriæ*
was being a little too enlightened when he called the reformer
a 'pacific man,' who with none of the religious fanaticism of a
Mohammed 'preached the Gospel peaceably' only. But he had
a good sense of Luther's knack of talking to the people in their
own style and on their own level, with a sound German down-
to-the-earth manner which he never disavowed. He said that
Luther's earnest studies differed from the speculative subtleties
of the Thomists 'as the art of husbandry from the whirlwind.'
He was 'an exceptional man,' 'who as a simple monk had
made light of the *savoir faire* of Councils' and 'one is no longer
tempted to believe that his writings are so bad as to be read with
distaste.' Evidently the attractiveness of the manner was as
persuasive as the depth of the matter. The portrait of this literary
Luther is somehow not quite genuine, but it had to be touched
up in order to make him presentable in Möser's century.

His letters are written in such a simple, solid style, they
provide not only truth but also distraction in their minute
detailing of his character. Erasmus, a reliable judge in æsthetical
matters, . . . could not deny him his consideration, and the

Jesuit Paul Besnier stated publicly that he wrote with a clarity that illuminated his whole achievement. If one lends an ear to Remond de Florimond and Varillas, the greatest thinker history has ever known, Nature appears to have endowed him with the *finesse* of an Italian joined with a German physique; and on one ever possessed in a higher degree the art of knowing all the intricacies of the heart, nor preaching with more fervour; finally the *finesse* of his style was second only to his amiable conversation. . . . Pope Leo X also recognized his fine mind. Maximilian and Charles did him equal justice. . . . So he lacks only your consideration, Monsieur, which I value next to that of emperors and popes.

Neither earlier nor later, but only in the eighteenth century, could that be written. A man approaches history and its heroes with his own criterion, never wholly ridding himself of his assumptions. For Möser, Luther's character was an accumulation of higher qualities only shaded off by a few weaknesses—and weaknesses there were bound to be, ' for he is man and was a monk.'

Literary character-study was a favourite pastime in the eighteenth century. Möser found the great man's passion and heart most admirable. ' Providence gave him fiery passions, the driving power of high virtues—noble pride, courage to go out in opposition to the clergy, a spirit at once impetuous and tolerant enough to turn the necessary storms to good account. . . .' And precisely his vehemence, which lesser minds frequently mistook for power complex, was an excellence. ' Whoever can distinguish between vices and passions is assured that a man without passion can be neither a rogue of mark nor a great man.' Möser caught a breath of that great wild spirit of Luther's—but lost it again: ' although Luther was a reformer, he was neither fanatical nor enthusiastic.'

Without being peculiar or rudely pedantic, his conversation was stimulating, his humour lively, his retorts powerful and well-placed and his table-talk very diverting. He ate well and almost always in the company of learned persons or some skilled craftsman such as Lucas Cranach, the most famous painter of his time. He often held concerts, accompanying himself, composing and playing the lute. And finally he was a theologian who could have stood up for himself in our own century without making his brethren blush.

His lack of restraint in dealing with his opponents attracted censure both in his own time and later. Möser remarked that a man whose greatness soared so high above the normal could not be expected to be as tamely correct in behaviour as the average man, and as the last word on the subject presumably, quoted a few lines in French alleged to be from Alexander Pope:

> *J'aime mieux un auteur sublime et véhément*
> *Qui tombe quelquefois, mais toujours noblement,*
> *Que ces rimeurs craintifs gênés dans leur justesse,*
> *Où, si rien ne déplait, rien aussi n'intéresse.* . . .

(b) THE EFFECTS OF THE REFORMATION

Such was the rehabilitation of Luther: an enumeration of human characteristics taken out of their religious and historical context, evaluated from an eighteenth-century angle and directed at making a good impression on Voltaire.

The two main achievements of this great personality were a successful population policy and the adaptation of religion to the requirements of State and society.

Möser started from the assumption that the ' monasterial age ' had an enormous debit account outstanding at the expense of the human race. The institution of the cloister was an evil for human society. Monastic life not only slighted the ' rights of nature ' but also tended ' to the total elimination of the species man.' Celibacy brought emigration to a standstill and reduced the population of Europe more than all the scourges of heaven— plague, hunger and war. Luther stood out as an heroic champion of the human race deserving a monument ' *ob conservatum genus humanum,*' for effectively calling a halt to the dwindling of populations. Möser calculated that the abolishing of about 4,000

monasteries had won the world a round 27 million people by
the eighteenth century, every monastery yielding thirty heads,
fifteen marriageable pairs, with an average of four children each;
in nine generations, 15 million people—not including those
'whom the Reformation prevented from consecrating themselves to their own destruction, who, at the same rate, would
produce in eight generations a progeny of more than twelve
millions.' From these calculations he concluded that the colonial
and commercial conquest of the world overseas—' trade in India
and the settlement of barren regions'—could never have occurred
on such a large scale, ' if the dissolution of the monasteries had
not permitted the birth of those millions of sailors and colonists
which Indian trade costs the European nations day by day.'

   The figures are, of course, wildly inaccurate. The first great
colonizing lands, Spain and Portugal, colonized without dissolv-
ing their monasteries. It was typical of the mercantile spirit of
the day to calculate the welfare of a state on a count of heads
and it shows how far the secularization of thought had gone,
when this mercantile scale of values could be used to weigh up
the pros and cons of the Reformation. Quantitative speculations
did not stop short of the spiritual field, but the Reformation had
a vital core which eluded Justus Möser's calculating mind. The
Reformation was the beginning of the enlightenment, on this he
agreed with most of his contemporaries. Luther's task had been to
enlighten the world and the Church, and he came into the world
in 1483 at the right moment. To some extent that was his luck,
the campaign that made him world famous was only possible
then. In the eighteenth century it would have been much harder
tor him, he could not have expected to find so much scope, for
' the Church is enlightened once for all and needs no more
torches.' Such was the absolute assumption of superiority of the
time—a well-ordered time, in the van of progress, to some
degree already perfect. But Möser saw the onset of progress in
Luther's efforts to ' revive the good and holy doctrine of the
early Church, to purify morals and apply them to general world
welfare.' Of the religion purified by Luther he stated, ' more
than everything else it is of service to the best in the State.'

He praised Luther for promoting unity in the State; 'to the honour of his doctrine,' there was no single Protestant State where 'physical and moral unity' was not the *dernier ressort*. Proudly he claimed:

> Our public worship is dependent on our ruler. He has the power to lay down the dogma of his Church in accordance with the basic laws of the State. But the final decision rests with our conscience alone, which leaves everyone free to go to heaven in his own chosen way.

The 'revival of early Church teaching by the Reformation' was a flourish automatically appended to every mention of Luther and his work. In the eighteenth century it was often synonymous with 'improvement of morals,' plus Möser's clause:—'and their application to the general well-being of the world'; with morals went politics in Lutheran districts where the State was in charge of the spiritual welfare of its subjects. Freedom of conscience was secularized into tolerance, freedom of belief, freedom of thought. On this point Justus Möser is as good a proof as Johann Salomo Semler that Church dogma and personal piety had nothing more to do with one another. The former was purely formal, a matter of State approval or assent; the latter left the individual with no spiritual obligations at all.[1]

When King Frederick II ridiculed Luther and Möser rushed to his rescue, we need not necessarily conclude that Möser understood Luther better than the king did. Neither had any idea of the real motives behind the Reformation, both were equally strangers to it. The King of Prussia had much the same views as the State Secretary of Osnabrück on the State Church, the utility of ethics, and religious individualism—fundamentally

[1] Möser considered that the moral direction of all orders in a State was necessary through a dogmatic religion based on revelation. His motive for thinking so was strongly pedagogical. He valued very highly the obligations established through dogmatic religion. Both the individual in reflecting on religious matters and the population as a whole were thus kept under discipline. For further evidence, cf. Justus Möser's "Letter to the Vicaire Savoyard, c/o M. Jean-Jacques Rousseau," in collected works published by B. R. Abeken, Vol. 5.

the very ideas that prevailed over old Lutheranism within theology itself. Freedom of personal conviction, claimed under the heading of freedom of conscience, allowed for the acceptance or rejection of any ideas on a purely personal estimation. What the point of view adopted was—whether more rational, or tending to belief—and whether one was a Christian or a free-mason, was now a matter of secondary importance.

Both King Frederick and Justus Möser were keen students of history, and both unwittingly demonstrate how far a critical estimation of events and a summing up of characters throw light on the personality and time of the writer, rather than on the historical period under consideration.

CHAPTER VII

HERALDS OF A NEW AGE : HERDER AND HAMANN

1. JOHANN GOTTFRIED HERDER

THE REVALUATION OF CHRISTIAN PRINCIPLES CONTINUES

HERDER was the son of an Evangelical precentor and himself a theologian. He was grateful to Luther for his Bible readings and his practical pastoral work, from which he took tips for his own work. He enjoyed quoting him and wrote a good deal about him but lost his urge to write a whole book in Weimar, we are told, and a work he sketched in 1792, ' Luther, a teacher of the German nation,' got no further. But he published the short introduction to it in the *Letters for the Advancement of Humanity* (18th in the 2nd collection). What he most loved was the human Luther powerfully possessed by his faith, the genial whirlwind of a prophet.

(a) ' OUR HEART-QUICKENING LUTHER '

Herder shared the general *Aufklärung* attitude to Luther to a large extent, not excluding complacency at belonging to an age at a much more advanced stage of progress. Though no lover of pure rationalism, Herder gave his whole-hearted assent to things as they were, and Luther was herald and precursor of the enlightenment; he had prepared the way for proper understanding and philosophy, freed humanity from the yoke of a papacy of blackest hue, battled successfully for the right of free thinking and independent belief, against dogma and theological indoctrination. Herder adopted as his own the *Aufklärung* axiom, that the uninhibited use of reason was an outcome of Luther's fight against the Church.

The main points held in common with his contemporaries were: Luther as a factor in the process of progress in world history; Luther as starting-point of progress and enlightenment; as father of freedom of thought as against prejudice, ignorance, and superstition; as father of individualism in religion.

(i) *The unique personality*

At the age of twenty-nine Herder broke out in eulogies:

> Simple, untaught Luther [he cried], how dear was God's word to thee! how thou didst love the people! from thy own belief and feeling, urged by the word of God, urgently in its cause speaking, writing, translating, and where knowledge failed, happily, adorably faltering on. . . . God's messenger to the people! Bearer and interpreter of the word for the world and for posterity! Prophet! Yea, prophet! . . .

The great advantage of the reformers was that they ' looked upon the cause of religion as a practical life-work.' But Herder missed the basic Christian-mindedness of Luther and the whole Reformation movement, and showed himself here too a son of his time, secularizing religion and making it ' natural.' In his work *Of Cognisance and Perception*: *The Two Principal Powers of the Human Soul* (1778), he returned again and again to the idea of genius, its growth and outbreak, and had no qualms in using Luther as much as Cæsar and Raphæl as samples. Montesquieu, Sarpi, Luther and Cæsar, named in a single breath, were so much confirmation of his theory that in certain sorts of genius the bud bursts comparatively late. A long inner strife full of dark unrest and yearning towards a new world had to take place in the ' genius created for action,' before powers were focused to the outward act, as might be seen from the example of Correggio, Luther and Raphael: ' Already in Luther the lawyer and monk, there slumbered all the tinder that awaited Tetzel's spark: the same active dark urge urged him into the monastery and martyred him with himself: already the future man, now a monk. . . .'

(ii) *The national note*

It is easy to show in what respect Herder was a man of his time. He was, however, not bound to its spirit, rather he tended to transform it, even to sweep on to further stages not always consonant with the lines most preconized. The Luther he stressed more than anyone had hitherto done, was the national hero and son of the soil, and he was fond of buckling the reformer's religious mandate with a mandate to the nation. In later middle age Herder wrote: ' Luther was a powerful mind, a true prophet and preacher of our fatherland. He first gave the classical book-language of the Germans its set form; all his writings are full of heart and courage. And his few hymns breathe German vigour . . .'

In an early study of new German literature (1767) he called Luther the man who had ' awoken and unbound that sleeping giant, the German language,' and ' roused a whole nation to think and feel.' He was ' the greatest master of translation in our language,' and is responsible for the formation of a ' public for popular literature in Germany . . .' This ' great patriotic man ' was prophet, messenger of God chosen from among the people, and teacher of the German nation, all in one. To the question, What did he teach? the answer was to some extent that of the *Aufklärung* in general: he taught the free mode of thinking and enquiring. Whence Herder's plea: ' Leave us his mode of thinking, even his household words and his home-truths so roundly said are fit for use and application in our time.'

Now when he said Luther roused his nation to think and feel, Herder was thinking of his own day: the reigning optimism and self-satisfaction were not shared by Herder (except at moments). Luther served as a stick to beat his times with: ' Great Luther was a clear resounding canon—resounding to infinity !— for the reviving of the wilting powers of perception. But in head and heart he saw infirm times ahead, warned of them—and they came! And one infirmity succeeded another: head-sway, heart-sway.' But in Luther's writings there reigned ' such sound understanding with such strength of courage and honest warmth of heart, that, quailed by the cold quibbling of later times, I often turned to him for refreshment.' At moments Luther was the soaring genius of the German people. Once he called to him in exaltation as to a spirit of the underworld:

Noble Shade, forgive that I have troubled thy spirit and borrowed sometimes hard but always vital words from thy lips and thy writings. I borrowed them to good purpose, to stem the seething spirit of my time, for excesses rule on both sides and not all can find the middle way. Become once more the Teacher of thy nation, its Prophet and Preacher, it may be that Germany, princes, nobles, court and people, will hear thy voice, with its truth clear as noonday, its tone and sound as persuasive as it can be terrible and fearful. Leave for another time the tenderer words from thy heart-inspired and heart-imparting lips. . . .

This made of Luther a sort of trusted Eckhart whose function was to admonish and warn and help Germany in times of danger. His regard for the nation was preferred to his regard for the Gospel—a precedent that was not without posterity in the nine-teenth century, and a further sign of the secularization of the age. The enlightenment was inimical to myth and irrationality, and behold, in the most pregnant minds of the nation Luther was now back in the realm of myth—but as *hero*, like Charles the Great, or later Bismarck. A figure belonging not to *Christian* but to *national* mythology; utterly remote from sixteenth- and seventeenth-century Protestantism with its Luther as the flying angel of the *Apocalypse*.

(iii) *Humanity and Theology*

Depreciation, confusion and ruin had befallen the ancient hold of religion on the souls of men. But after the *Aufklärung* there came a partial religious revival. What revived, however, was an attitude to religion in a general sense, and not at all Christianity in a biblical sense. The cause of this is that religion was sought not objectively in revelation but subjectively in feeling and intimation.

A sharp wedge had been driven between theology and ' religion.' Herder called the contrasting of ' indoctrination and religion ' an outstanding achievement of the great theologians of Germany, from Luther and Melanchthon up to his own contemporaries Semler, Teller and Henke. In their name he resisted all attempts ' to give the Bible a meaning such that its figments about an old story be reconstituted as religion.' A right-doing man can be without indoctrination but never without religion. ' Genuine religion cannot be without right-doing, and inmost right-doing is religion, which is indeed how it is known.' A right-doing man practises religion when he does his work conscientiously; there is no doctrine but has its worth, ' he picks the best out of all; but none may take the place of religion.'

We see now how Herder could contradict himself and get away with it; nonetheless when he gave whole-hearted support to Luther's views without relinquishing his own standpoint, he was indulging in a highly one-sided interpretation of the reformer. In his letters on the study of theology, he advised students to take the doctrine of justification, the ' corner-stone,' as guide through Luther's works, but did not hesitate elsewhere sharply to criticize strict Lutheran teaching on justification. ' After the great man's death, not only were his truest helpers insulted, scolded, persecuted and calumniated as Synergists, but henceforth a man undergoing a so-called conversion was to remain a dolt and blockhead. Dolts and blockheads there were on the way to conversion . . . inevitably. . . .' He was blind to the problem that beset Luther and the reformers, grace versus freedom in the act of justification. ' Fortunately time has sunk in the broad stream of oblivion all these senseless biblical aberrations, as well as the controversy as to the diverse graces. . . . May the hand wither that would seek to retrieve them.' That for Luther religion was firmly anchored in them he would never sanction—a further consequence of the contemporary separation of ' indoctrination' and ' religion,' which Herder reflected back on to the past.

The heart of the matter, the Protestant cause, he saw not in Luther's doctrine but in his general attitude. The ' great advantage' of the reformers was that they ' looked upon the cause of religion as an active life-work' and spoke ' from a full heart' of the Bible. Feeling, will, fervour work in Luther against cold formalism. Now that may have been a side-issue of the

Reformation, it was not its heart and soul as Herder would have it. He liked to contemplate Luther as a sort of second self: a champion of the right to existence of all that is lively and individual, as against the mechanization and inorganic rationalization of life. Anyone who wants to know what faith is, he wrote in his theological letters, should read Luther. ' Re-birth and faith is the principle, the true magic power, the living spark of a new creation for a new existence; not philosophic enlightenment.' Faith was a form of temperamental energy, surging from irrational sources and lifting a man out of himself; more or less the antithesis of the vaunted power of reason.

Now in the first verse of the eleventh chapter of the *Epistle to the Hebrews* we read: ' What is faith? It is that which gives substance to our hopes, which convinces us of things we cannot see.' Here faith is brought into relation with that to which it tends. And we know that Luther's faith was clearly set on its object. There is no inkling of it in Herder. To Christianity it was a grace, a supernatural gift ' outpoured,' but to Herder an indetermined principle of ' liveliness,' connected with spontaneity and naturalness and humanity full-grown.

It was this natural conception of faith (' natural ' as distinct from the Christian ' spiritual ') that he attributed gratuitously to Luther.

A similar distortion appears in the few remarks of Herder's on Luther's *De servo arbitrio*. The Protestants of the enlightenment could not stand the book at any price. Not only because it was directed against Erasmus (the author of *De libero arbitrio*), whom they honoured as their mentor, but also because it agreed ill with their practical kind of piety that more or less excluded will-power. Herder as a young man stood out in his own way for non-freedom of the will. Luther meant in a strictly spiritual sense the powerlessness of man in the process of justification. Herder for his part based it on feeling and interpreted it as Luther's natural experience of man's limitations, explaining freedom of will as a deliberate trespass beyond the limitations imposed on man, which is to say that freedom of will is *hubris*, non-freedom is cultivated self-control. Then in a remarkable inverse ratio he also described freedom of the will as servitude, and servitude of the will as the beginning of freedom. A formula expresses what he meant: freedom of will: arbitrariness: ' cow-like servitude of the senses ' ; servitude of the will: feeling of human non-freedom: ' the first germ of freedom.' Behind these thoughts loomed the model personality of Goethe's time, man winning through to true inner freedom by imposing limitations on himself. Herder was a little over thirty at the time and a theologian; the verve and unconcern with which he developed this ideal personality out of elements of Luther's doctrine of the will are cause for reflection on the prodigious curve described by Lutheran theology from its starting-point to Herder. The individual, at one time set God-wards, was now turned in on himself. Herder enquired whether it was not really the first germ of freedom to feel the bonds that bound one.

The strongest free-est men [he replied] feel them most deeply and strive further; fools, slaves born for the prison, sneer at them and, filled with high dreams, remain prostrate in the mire. Luther, with his book *De servo arbitrio*, was and will be understood by the very few. . . . Why? because people do not feel like him and struggle upwards. Luther's servitude of the will was to the semi-wise an offence, to the semi-virtuous folly. And this very doctrine shows Luther's deep feeling for the bonds of humanity. . . . The bird fancies itself free in its net-room and the bird-catcher never for a moment doubts that it is bound fast in servitude. It raises a man to a high level to be intellectually and morally aware of the net.

The freedom which Luther denied, as against Erasmus, consisted in a man doing what he was in a position to do but ought not to do. Thus when Adam sinned, it was out of freedom. Had he not sinned, he would have refrained out of a proper sense of the limitations of his state. What Luther conceived as an objective powerlessness, from which Christ alone could redeem, became for Herder subjectively a virtue in man: ' to be aware of the net.' The whole idea had been pulled down on to the natural plane and become ethical instead of religious.

How Herder ' humanized' yet a third point of Lutheran theology shall be shortly told. Here again, he only meant to explain Luther. The second article of the creed—'. . . and in Jesus Christ . . .' he expounded ' as closely to Luther as possible,' and advised the readers of his letters on the study of theology to do the same.

One has here the best opportunity to avoid very common but nonetheless erroneous ideas about the supreme power of the devil, from whom Christ has redeemed us, and about the magical power of his blood and many other unworthy mis- conceptions which must be corrected. The satisfaction and sacrifice of Jesus appear here from the plainest point of view as those of a saving friend, who hazarded his whole self, life and death, on my behalf and who is now out of justice and love my lord.

It was a pointer in the same direction when Herder spoke of Luther's nearness to St. Paul's understanding of the Lord's Supper and praised Luther for " feeling darkly the more pregnant significance of the whole act," and the Pauline teaching he inter- preted as ' a symbolic custom of genuine union between men and their invisible friend, and among one another.' Christ was thereby humanized too, for although reverent and affectionate words were found to tell of his mildness and friendship for man, there was no mention of him as God, of his lordship with God the Father in the unity of the Holy Spirit in eternity, which was for Luther alpha and omega.

In fact Herder laid it open to question whether Christ freed us from the power of Satan, thereby leaving the fact of original sin hanging in the air, though Bible revelation shows it as the great decisive event between the creation and the redemption. Likewise, according to the Evangelists and the *Apocalypse*, we are redeemed by Christ's blood shed for us and this mystery is at the heart of the sacrament of the Eucharist. We are expressly and explicitly directed to believe in the mysterious power of the blood of Christ. How strange then that a theologian should tell us to beware of erroneous ideas on the magic power of this blood, to correct them, and to substitute the idea of the ' saving friend ' !

The process is by now familiar: original Christian ideas, which the *Aufklärung* often misinterpreted and formalized, were revived and given new depth by Herder, but they were transformed into human, individual, this-worldly ideas, and divested of their divine character. We have always to remember that the distorted forms of these ideas were transposed back on to Luther, or were even supposedly gleaned from a study of his works. There was nothing else for it: Luther had to be distorted, otherwise there was no making anything of him.

(b) THE REFORMATION AND HERDER'S IDEAS

For eighteenth-century rationalists, the Reformation meant that major turning-point in history when the domination of prejudice, error, ignorance, and religious coercion was overcome through the victorious advance of reason, independent criticism, ' truth ' (as they repeated indefatigably), and tolerance; when political, economic and spiritual servitude ceased and freedom began for conscience and State.

Herder took it all for granted, made these notions his own and carried them on to further conclusions. The Reformation was to be envisaged as the type of the ' great world changes,' freedom was its principle.

(i) *The Reformation as Revolution*

Impervious as he probably was to the real meaning of Protestantism, Herder was all the more sensitive to the energies let loose by the movement. He observed their revolutionary effect on the social conditions of the day, sweeping away old forms of order, setting up new ones. A consideration of the origins of historical change gave birth to the idea of the Reformation as a standard example by which to demonstrate the phenomenon. It was an early attempt at morphological history. He observed the sequence of events and looked for an underlying organic principle. World history appeared as a process of birth and growth which he could elucidate by means of illustrations and notions taken from natural science, demonstrating that principle eluding all calculation, which drives on the course of events and leads to results utterly different from those men plan. For this principle that emerges victorious over all human plans and aims, and throws overboard all schemes and reckonings, he had various names.

If we enter further into the conditions of origin of all so-called world-illuminations: we find it again. Now in larger sweep, now small. Chance, Fate, Godhead! It was tiny things that started every reformation, far remote from the immensely great plan they became involved in later; and moreover, whenever there was a grandly-conceived human plan at the beginning, it came to nothing.

Herder introduced as dissident voice a ' mild philosopher,' who inquired why, instead of letting the human spirit go on at its own quiet pace, the Reformation was allowed through passion to degenerate into revolution—and supplied his own answer: ' while such quiet advancement of the human spirit in the improvement of the world is little else but a figment of our imagination, and never the way of God in nature.'

The irrational force that made history was nature and godhead at once. It was at work not only in history but also in the vegetable world. The way plants develop was a symbol of the historical process. Growth remained mysterious.

The grain falls into the earth, there it lies torpid; then comes the sun to awake it: it bursts: the cells swell powerfully apart: it thrusts through the soil—and thus to blossom, to fruition—even the horrid fungus hardly grows as you imagine it. The cause of every reformation was always—even such a small seed of grain falling silently into the earth—not worth mentioning: men had had it there for a long time, saw it not, paid it no heed—though tastes, manners and a world of customs were to be altered and newly-fashioned by it.—Is that possible without revolution, without passions, and movement?

Parallel events to Luther's Reformation were the discoveries of Roger Bacon, Galileo, Descartes and Leibniz: ' When they came upon their discovery, all was quiet: it was a ray of light—but the discoveries were to break through, alter opinions, change the world—then was storm and flame.' Significant in the Reformation was something typical underlying all movements, nothing intrinsic about the Reformation itself. What mattered was not the particular course of development but the general character of historical turning-points, a character comparable to certain functions of nature, in its violence and cruelty cataclysmic. Herder advanced his theory with some complacency and not much forethought, and was pulled up short by the ticklish problem of humanity in the toils of organic history.

Everyone knows what all reformers have always been accused of: when they take a step forward they leave gaps behind, rouse dust and distress ahead and trample the innocent underfoot. The reformers of the last centuries are not exempt, far from it. Luther! Gustavus Adolphus! Peter the Great! What other three have made more changes in modern times? —Have their successes (some of them unforeseen) always contributed to an undeniable increase in happiness for their posterity? Who, knowing the subsequent history, will not sometimes doubt it?

Logic required history seen as a nature-bound process to take place within the sphere of necessity and law, with humanity as executive handy-man. An organic system of laws not susceptible to rational explanation replaced the rational system, with man performing historic acts as though under invisible stage directions. History as a whole became the work of the stage-manager, not of man. The organic process in history was as necessary as its counterpart in nature, for neither one nor the other could escape from the mysterious power of the laws that rule it. Thus Luther was not the author of the Reformation, but the servant of it, more often unconsciously than consciously. This ' excellent ignorant monk ' pulled off something that all the emperors, kings, cardinals and lords of the world could not do.

And that starting from tiny things, himself thinking anything but so far ahead, with means with which, seen through
the eyes of our time, philosophically speaking, nothing like it
could be done! Mostly himself doing the least, except that
he started others off, roused reformers in all lands. . . . Thus
came about what came about—world-wide change! How often
had other Luthers earlier arisen and—come to nothing. . . .

Why was it Luther's fate to be different? Because now

it is spring-time; the earth lies open, the sun fosters life, and
a thousand new growths appear—Man, thou wast never aught
but a small blind tool, and reluctantly that.

Herder as a younger man tried to come to terms with the
super-personal element in history. In the Reformation what
struck him was *der Gang Gottes in der Natur*, 'God as a force in
nature.' This was no revelation, but the very essence of evolution
within history, responsible for the process of 'becoming,'
for how the new thing was born, unfolded, throve. Herder
could have chosen other historic revolutions. The Reformation
was not in any case the main point of interest, but the law of
historical change, just as when Herder compared Luther to Sarpi,
Raphael and Correggio, it was not for Luther's sake, but to
demonstrate the break-through of genius. What remained of
Luther and the Reformation? The spirit gone, the singularity
gone, they were reduced to a mere historical event.

(ii) *Freedom a principle of the Reformation*

As he grew older, Herder was inclined to see the whole
history of mankind in all its forms and periods ruled by the law
of growth and evolution—a single coherent comprehensive
process of becoming. Its goal was perfected humanity, and
throughout its duration each individual and each nation was to
bring to cultural expression and harmonious fulfilment whatever
talents and abilities were there, for the benefit and enjoyment of
all concerned. Thus history had a goal and moved on towards
it, and natural organic evolution had a spiritual meaning. Human
endeavour carried evolution on beyond the scope of mere

natural growth, hence its sense of direction. By linking historical morphology to progress Herder humanized his concept of history.

Freedom was the principle that entered modern history with the Reformation and Protestantism—a progressive and at the same time a spiritual principle. Herder defined it as freedom of every form of expression: of conscience, of conviction and of conduct—the latter, in relation to faith, understood as independence of the natural moral man from codes and creeds. The greatest achievement of the Reformation was that it drew the line as between Bible-reading and theology. The Protestant not only could but should make free use of the Bible, and could tolerate no prescribed codes in matters of doctrine and interpretation. . . . Ecclesiastical authority was on principle contrary to freedom and Herder revered Luther for overthrowing it. Some of Herder's expressions are reminiscent of sixteenth-century controversy: scholasticism, Aristotle, councils, Church fathers were all set up against the Bible just as in the days of the old reformers. But the likeness is more apparent than real, for in Herder the principle of freedom issuing so strongly from the Reformation is of the two the older: the Reformation was the child of freedom. Man when he is not marked with the mark of freedom is not man. Freedom is a mark of his nature, and the Reformation derived from the nature of man. 'The human spirit must have freedom,' he wrote in the letters on the study of theology, 'even though he misuse it too. The word of God is his to understand and expound as he see fit and proper, even though he expound it wrong.' It was at once as historical fact and as natural phenomenon that the Reformation broke out into freedom, casting off the chains of servitude.

'The right of humanity, freedom' justified the Reformation, and from freedom issued all that is called Reformation, wholesome religion, salvation and truth; from its base arose 'the Protestant Churches . . ., sound reason, all the ready virtues of the heart, all the successful issue of further endeavour.'

The freedom conducive to religion and salvation was, much as he had deduced it from Luther's *De servo arbitrio*, a self-limitation of the autonomous individuality from within, without external compulsion. 'The spirit is of the nature of Lutheranism, as it is of the nature of Christianity: free conviction, examination and self-determination. Without this spirit of freedom all is or will be but moribund. . . .' Imposed 'enclosure' as Herder called it ('so far may freedom go and no further') should not exist at all. 'True freedom must limit itself from within, and truly it limits itself more sharply than any enclosure because it only does so from innermost conviction after choosing and testing.' The worst anti-Lutheran was the man who wanted to put an end to this freedom in Lutheranism or in another Protestant communion. 'He discards the very principle of the Reformation . . . he damns to perdition Luther and all his followers and all true men of former times lying in their graves.'

(iii) *The Reformation as midwife to Humanity*

'The Reformation established everywhere the principle of the free use of reason,' and introduced an improved concept of freedom of conscience and good works suitable 'for application by men and citizens,' and superseding the authority of the clergy. This led to a free expansion of schools, learning, philosophy, politics and tolerance, throughout Europe. Forward-driving forces, explosive matter, attracted Herder. In the Reformation he saw his contemporary Europe in germ, striving towards complete humanity. The set-backs, controversies, peasants' wars and so on left him untouched. They were imperfections, relics of an age outlived, where conflicts took place in the dark because 'clear principles' were absent. Humanity budding out in all directions after the Reformation was what aroused his enthusiasm. But these effects and principles of Herder's, supposed blossoms of the Reformation, were the more obviously of quite other extraction, the more Herder identified them with his ideal of humanity.

> A spirit of advancement is in it,
> the true realization of the human mind,
> the true realization of human emotions and heart . . .

—and its goal was perfection in this world for man and the community. Humanity was advanced by the Reformation, for

' the spirit of mutual hatred among nations grew weaker ' and ' general aims for humanity were set afoot.' The interrelations of states must gain ' through real Protestantism, even without its name.' For free activity of mind, heart and emotions was bound to result in increasing harmony among nations—in contrast to ' all that was oppressive, useless, meaningless in Catholicism '— and ' religion will be generally felt as at once a human and a State concern.'

Humanity freed from constraint and thrown back on to its own devices was to transform the world into a peaceful cosmos merely by bringing to full expansion its own noble powers. There was to be a general hatching and developing of talents, but never at the neighbour's expense: all would grow and thrive in harmony together.

What had the Reformation to do with all this? Herder said it made people ripe to enter into the stage of peaceful growth. It introduced tolerance into religion. This was all the more necessary as the organic evolution of individual and national idiosyncrasies was not compatible with the existence of an intolerant confession. Hence mutual tolerance among Churches was a *sine qua non*. A man's religion should never be submitted to the judgement of other men. The unity of religion consisted in devotion to ' common utility, reason, truth.' And this too Herder claimed as an effect of the Reformation.

(iv) Luther, Protestantism and National Religion

The unity of religion was not on any account to be established by interfering in the form and nature of religions as they stood— consecrated by time and place; things must go on as they were, in their own way. There was no need to do anything about it, religion was in any case simply a matter of behaviour and disposition—' right-doing '—and a creed was irrelevant. Herder's religion of free humanity was not bound to the word of God at all. It consisted almost wholly in the culture of nationality and individuality incumbent on everyone as person and member of a nation. Nothing could be more remote from St. John's ' one shepherd and one fold,' and the question remains whether there was any compatibility left between Herder's religion and Christianity. 'Luther,' he said, 'neither could nor would put our minds under the yoke of traditional forms and words. Christ himself neither could nor would. He, the freer of man's mind, not its tyrant or gaoler. The Apostles neither could nor would. . . .' Dogma was excluded, evolution was introduced. The Apostles did not formulate articles of belief, they saw 'their time as a time for beginning to build, and the building was to be carried on with increasing knowledge and perfection. They saw Christianity in its infancy, and one day it will and must reach perfect manhood.'

Herder was thinking of the passage in *Ephesians* iv, 11–16, where 'perfect manhood' is 'that maturity which is proportioned to the completed growth of Christ.' This cannot be understood except in relation to the Holy Trinity. Herder, however, applied it to his system of organic becoming. It is not at all unthinkable that he took his religion of humanity for an evolution of Christianity 'through increasing knowledge and perfection.'

In one of his later books, the fourth volume of *Adastrea* (1802), he studied the remarkable relationship in which he saw Christianity, Protestantism, national religion, individual piety, and the peace of nations on earth, all bound together and interdependent. He imagined a conversation 'On National Religions,' between two men, Dietrich and Winnfried, Dietrich remarking:

. . . The heart of man wants a religion he has felt himself, man's mind wants truth he has thought himself. You have certainly experienced how painful it is when truth is told untruthfully and living life put in dead formulæ; I too—to me it was as though a blooming virgin were clothed in cloths from tombs and masked in old masks.

Winnfried took up the idea as he always did, and Dietrich's questions came pat to give him his chance: the conversation might as well have been a monologue and was more like a sermon, or an interview.

Winnfried: Every conscience feels it. Hence the resistance of the nations when with their speech the religion of their fathers is taken from them. Hence, when after the long death-like sleep under the yoke of foreign words and customs human feeling re-awoke—the special rejoicing. Do you, Dietrich, know that German who brought back to his nation, with its authentic speech, its authentic religion, which is belief, faith, mind and heart?—Protestantism, against everything uncouth, everything foreign?

Dietrich: You mean Luther. Sad that the great man could not achieve what was so much to be desired, a Church of his nation, a German Church!

Winnfried: A German Church, Dietrich? That would have been unworthy of the great man. Observe what became of Henry VIII's English Church, or any other Church that cuts itself off from the rest: they rot alive. But religion, the pure free religion of conscience, mind and heart was what Luther intended for his Germans. And gave it them, however much his times may have abandoned it.

Dietrich: Unfortunately not all Germans. And his language is in many respects outworn.

Winnfried: Let it be rejuvenated! But it renews itself, continually, irresistibly. Is it nothing, do you suppose, that since he wrote, every German, when he wants to be read by the better part of the nation, must write as Evangelical, Protestant, Lutheran, even if he do it against his will? That parade of masks is over, aping foreign peoples and times. Protestantism against errors and superstition, every man to his own conviction, so must each man write, on pain of becoming a laughing-stock and not being read.

Dietrich: Suppose that none of our great men read German?

Winnfried: So much the worse for them. Whoever is ashamed of his own nation and his own tongue has torn asunder the bond that binds him to the nation—the religion of his people. I incline to believe that whoever now lays upon the altar of the fatherland pure intentions—to whatever effect they may be, and the power of his mind and heart, is continuing Luther's work and promoting national religion in the most exact sense of the word, that is, as conscientiousness and conviction.

Dietrich: A truly Protestant and Lutheran belief. And it was in that sense that you wished for national religions for all the peoples of the earth?

Winnfried: In that sense. For the peace of the world, for the cultivation of every nation in its main stem and in its branches. No foreign tongue or religion shall despotize over the speech and soul of any nation whatever. An over-shepherd for all human flocks, with a language the nation does not understand, ignorant of its innermost needs, will be unthinkable. Each nation flourishes like a tree from its own roots— and Christianity, which is true conviction towards God and man, is henceforth nought but the pure dew of heaven altering not at all a tree's own character and fruit, and de-naturalizing no human creature. Peace will reign on earth, peace! . . . (for in poetry, pleasure and custom nations are diverse).

Dietrich: Individuals too: so that in the long run each man will possess his own religion, just as he possesses his own heart, his own belief and speech.

Winnfried: And no other may pass judgement on what lies in the innermost heart of a man. . . .

Herder was in full agreement with Semler and Lessing that religion was a private matter, it was individual righteousness and disposition that counted. And to the question, what religion depended upon, he answered, upon man. More precisely, upon the heart of man, ' for it wants a self-felt religion.' And truth depended upon the mind of man, which ' wants a self-thought truth.'

What had all this to do with Luther? A great deal, said Herder: Luther having brought his people, with the ' genuine language,' ' genuine religion.' You denied Luther by being ashamed of your language and nation, and continued his work by offering up your good intentions and powers of mind and heart ' on the altars of the fatherland.' Humanity, world citizenship, freedom from every narrow nationalism were implied; for Herder, national religion was not a cult for its own sake but for the sake of humanity: a nation was a branch of the tree of humanity; humanity was an organism and its limbs were nations, and the healthy development of each contributed to the well-being of the whole.

The growth and cultivation of each national religion were fundamentally beneficial, so Herder understood, because he was firmly convinced that the various parts of humanity were harmoniously co-ordinated. Luther he hailed as the promoter of this harmony.

Among nations as among individuals, living together in harmony was the result of the still-continuing evolution of national religions, and Herder expected their further cultivation to bring about the peace of the world.

(c) HERDER'S RELIGION AND CHRISTIANITY

Protestantism ought to promote a better understanding among nations and must be a religion of tolerance, non-dogmatic, natural and human. It would be going too far to call this Christianity, nor is it easy to trace the points of contact.

If the individual had been shown the way to himself and nations had been shown the way to themselves, individual and nation were both to learn that the cultivation of their idiosyncrasies was religion. Language naturally played an important part, and Protestantism had performed an immense cultural function which it must continue to perform.

How different was the cultural function of the early mediæval Church, for instance. Then, a Christian culture was created by religion, that is, culture was Christianized. In Herder's scheme of things, culture was secularized, and he called this secularized culture, religion. Service to individual and national and human culture was Protestant religion. We learn how Protestantism

evolved into individualism, into a national idea in the framework
of humanity, into humanity itself; but we seldom hear what it
had to do with Christianity. The fact of the matter was, Christianity had evolved into Protestantism. When Herder said
Christianity, it is doubtful that he meant Christianity. His
religion was a ' dew from heaven ' but it did not release a man
from his nature tainted with original sin, nor confer on him as
in baptism a mark of holiness, clothing our first Adam with
the second Adam, raising us to rebirth in a world beyond
nature.

Where Herder saw self-development as the supreme good for
individual and nation, St. Paul[1] shows us all creation ' full of
expectancy,' ' waiting for the sons of God to be made known,'
for ' nature in its turn will be set free from the tyranny of corruption to share in the glorious freedom of God's sons. The whole
of nature, as we know, groans in a common travail all the while.'
We must be changed before we are made perfect: ' Here
is a secret I will make known to you : we shall all rise
again. . . .'[2]

In short, Herder's religion was one in which the seeds sown
by pietism and rationalism grew to luxuriant growth in amazing
union with his own ideas of the organic character of individuals
and nations and the genetic evolution of history. It had an
immense influence on the following century. Consisting as it
did of feeling and experience, conscious national clanship and
membership of humanity, it issued from human conditions and
not at all from the quite other conditions of God. It implied this-
worldly personal autonomy, not other-worldly personal dependence. It could not be at home with any Christian religion based
on revelation and a creed, directing its ultimate hopes to a life
beyond death.

Enhancing individualism, secularizing religion, raising secular
human activities to be religion, Herder produced an early sample
of the attitude that in many variations and denominations
became so familiar a factor of life in the nineteenth century and
after.

---

[1] *Romans* viii, 19-22.   [2] I *Cor.* xv, 51.

2. JOHANN GEORG HAMANN : THE REACTION

(a) RETURN TO LUTHER

Herder's debt to Kant, twenty years his senior, as well as to Johann Georg Hamann (1730–1788) is very considerable. Hamann was fourteen years his senior, an East Prussian as he was himself. Goethe set the fashion of dubbing him ' the Magus of the North ' and he was usually referred to as gloomy, obscure, confused, melancholy. Goethe had a high opinion of him and late in years seriously thought of bringing out or instigating an edition of his works. His connection with the Romantic Movement is a familiar chapter of the history of literature, and next to Herder he is its chief precursor. He remained in correspondence with his one-time pupil Herder all his life—a correspondence that yields a good deal of grist to our mill.

He held insignificant positions in the customs offices in Königsberg and had some difficulty in making ends meet for himself and his many dependants. During a stay in London, before he turned thirty, he underwent a conversion. He embarked on an intensive study of the Bible, reading it right through twice on end. A first-fruit of his conversion was his *Biblical Considerations of a Christian (Biblische Betrachtungen eines Christen)*, published posthumously.

With Lessing, Semler, Kant and Möser, he belonged to the generation that witnessed the rise of Prussia under Frederick the Great and came under the influence and domination of that monarch and of the *Aufklärung* in all its religious, philosophical and social nuances.

Like Herder, Hamann was a man of great individuality, and his relation to Luther was also a strongly personal one. But he stressed the geniality and powerful personality of the reformer less than his churchmanship and Christian spirit, particularly since his own conversion. He never lost sight of Luther's human qualities, which moved him profoundly. This may account for the fact of his reading Möser's letter to Voltaire ' with uncommon pleasure ' ten years after its appearance, in 1760, when he was thirty; finding in it nothing to quarrel with but rather a whole heap of his own ideas, as he wrote to his brother, urging him to read it too. What greatly pleased him was Möser's allusion to ' a passage of Voltaire's *Essay on Man* which showed considerable agreement with a passage of Luther's [on the human heart] . . . which I never tire of reading.' Apart from this, however, Hamann's opinions are remote from Möser's.

Not only did he think along quite different lines, his personal relationship to Luther was entirely different from that of the eighteenth-century men we have studied: he experienced this relationship as a challenge of vital concern to his soul and salvation. It never occurred to him to compare Luther's genius to Raphael's or Leibniz'. His work, he said, was the necessary equipment of a Christian, along with the Bible and hymn-book: ' What are Montaigne and Bacon, the idols of French *esprit* and English profundity, compared with him! '

The reformer was the servant of the Gospel and Hamann's chosen guide to Bible-Christianity. He termed him ' our Church Father.' His Bible-translation had for Hamann the authority of the Vulgate—a contrast indeed to Lessing, who in Luther's name demanded translation-rights for freethinkers and atheists. At thirty, Hamann announced that he was ' Lutherizing,' that he could never tire of reading the prefaces to the Psalms and to the *Romans*, that he read Luther with uncommon trust and had made up his mind to go right through his whole works. At fifty, suffering alike from attacks of gout and from the spirit of his *seculi*, Hamann not only read the Jena edition of Luther, Volumes I to VI, in six weeks, but as he told Herder, determined then and there to bring into general use the Walch edition, at that time the modern one. ' I soaked it up like a sponge,' he wrote to Herder, and in a letter to Göttingen: ' Luther's works are my main reading . . . my *pium desiderium*! my *ultimum visibile*! '

The quotations that on occasion amplify his comments let us see what Hamann chiefly revered in the reformer: it was the theologian, making known with power and cordiality the meeting-place where man comes face to face with God. It was, too, the expert on the human heart and the conditions of human life. To his friends Lindner and Behrens he tried to explain his conversion in words of Luther's own:

It is true [he wrote] I have done things that I myself find inexplicable . . . 'but this I will say, if you can see what I mean, I was not at all anxious to commit myself, and still less did I want to come in as a beginner. God has set these things in a place which all your oratory will never find, nor your philosophy, nor your politics; it is called Faith, containing all things which we can neither see nor grasp. To seek to make them visible, evident, and within our reach, as you do, is to reap heart-ache and lamentation, as you indeed have done, with no consent of ours.'—These are words of our Father Luther to Melanchthon.

Some lines of Luther's on the inconstancy of the human heart, which like a ship on high seas is driven hither and thither by the gale striking on it from all the points of the compass—a passage from the preface to the Psalms—fascinated Hamann as a young man to such a degree that he could not resist reading them over and over again. It was, he felt, his own experience. On June 30, 1780, he wrote to Johann Caspar Häfeli:

A few days before your kind letter came, I read in Luther ' of the knight Kondalo, on a narrow bridge, a load on his back; beneath, a sulphurous pool full of dragons, and one— coming towards him.' Commentary on *Matthew* VII. At that point I knew for certain I had found the key to myself.

Lessing and Herder had both laid claim to a spiritual affinity with Luther. They adopted him as their mentor: Luther was to guarantee *their* success. Hamann, on the contrary, wanted simply what Luther wanted: to stand at the foot of the Cross and be a servant of Christ. Hamann was not only conscious of affinity, he was actually near the reformer, in faith and in fact, knowing ' no other orthodoxy but our small Lutheran catechism.' Honouring Luther as Church Father, true teacher of the faith and exponent of Scripture, he contended against all Catholic views of Church and Church history, if out of tune with Lutheran views, and inclined to regard Lutheranism and Christianity, if not entirely as identical, at least as wholly in harmony. Obviously, it was the old Lutheran positions that he occupied. But he did not start inside, he had to fight his way in, overcoming the opposition of his times and his own private resistance; thus, all alone, he won through to the old faith-bound stronghold of orthodoxy, bringing into it fire and life.

Historically seen, the opposite number of Lutheranism had always been the papacy. In the eighteenth century the actual adversary of the Christian faith was the *Aufklärung*, known to contemporaries as the fashionable philosophy, or worldly wisdom —as the case might be. Eagerly pursuing his Luther readings, Hamann found his attention constantly drawn to the pope as Christ's adversary; and meanwhile, day in day out, he had every occasion to observe how the enlightened thought of his own time was opposed to Christ. The enemy was here the papacy, there the enlightenment: Hamann deduced that the enlightenment issued from the papacy. He readily termed it a new papacy. His own firm stand on the faith set him in radical opposition to the ' enlightened ' stand of his environment. Lively controversy ensued which enabled him to define his own position. But he kept to his predilection for dubbing his opponent, on Luther's warrant, ' papacy '—a term covering everything inimical to Christianity.

(b) HAMANN—CRITIC OF HIS TIMES

With ' papacy ' as a generic term to denote the moralizing philosophy and so-called ' natural ' religion of the time, Hamann laid bare the anti-Christian vein in contemporary thought, but ran full-tilt into the imperturbability of the lords of reason and the moralists, who from the heights of their superior wisdom looked down on the traditional faith as superstition. Thus despotism and unbelief came together in his mind in a single dominating idea embracing both the papacy and the enlightenment. In later life he stressed this connection more and more. In the ' Hierophantic Letters ' of 1775, he proposed the following ' suppositions ' to the judgement of his readers:

Whether the unbelief of theism [he certainly means deism] and the superstition of the papacy do not at bottom have one common meaning and purpose and effect, pursuing apparently contrary but in reality united ends: resistance to the most holy faith of Christians. . . .

Whether theism as a natural son of the papacy and likewise its fiercest foe in hearth and home, does not boast of a hierarchy and like the papacy contain unbelief *in petto*. . . .

Whether Christianity is not required by its Founder to bear the cross of a double shame and be slandered for superstition and unbelief by Jews and heathen, theists and papists, to their own damnation.

A decade later he discarded the prudent disguise of ' suppositions ' and declared openly that despotism and a moralizing form of superstition were about to unite to set up a new papacy. ' Catholicism,' he said, ' is nothing but despotism. Instead of the Roman one, a metaphysical moralizing one has arisen, with its seat in the very place where the hue and cry was raised over the papacy.' Its other distinguishing traits were infallibility, disregard for Holy Scripture, and salvation by works.[1] These rubrics were to cover Roman Catholicism, the philosophy of Spinoza, pantheism and the whole philosophical contraband in ' reason.' In his own century he saw ' man's work ' take precedence of faith, and attacked, explicitly or implicitly, in the name of Luther. He stopped short nowhere, calling Kant's ' goodwill '—' another phantom of the brain,' alongside the old idol of ' pure reason.' He wrote to Herder: ' That Kant is one of our keenest minds even his enemy must allow, but unluckily this cleverness is his undoing, much as Lessing's is his.' Lessing's *Education of the Human Race* was merely ' the old leaven of our fashionable philosophy,' born of ' ignorance of the true spirit of the Reformation.' He had the courage to stand out boldly in defence of the Christian point of view against the author of *Nathan* and the editor of the *Fragments*.

[1] Cf. letter to F. H. Jacobi, 2.3.1786.

In *reason* as enthroned in his day he saw the true enemy of faith and condemned it accordingly. In its name religion was distorted and natural religion had become generally accepted, though in natural religion ' there is hardly a mention of the Messias.'—' To me, natural religion is, like natural speech, sheer nonsense, an *ens rationis*.' He was among the first to see that what was ' obvious ' to the *Aufklärung* was in reality nothing of the sort. He saw deeper and further. He was aware of problems of which the spirit of the age had no idea. The *Aufklärung* turned its critical scrutiny onto everything except itself. It queried everything except its own ' natural reason,' proudly so called in contrast to ' belief.' Hamann perceived that its self-adulation was without a shadow of justification. As he expressed it in a lapidary phrase: ' What is called natural religion is just as problematical and polemical as revelation.' Thus he cleared the way for the revival of much that the *Aufklärung* had suppressed: the non-rational powers of feeling and longing, of the unknown, of tradition and the mystery of organic growth;—powers which in Romanticism broke out explosively. Hamann contested the right of reason to be set up as universal judge and showed up the arrogance of this one-judge attitude. But he termed this arrogance ' papacy.'

By showing up ' natural religion ' and the worship of reason in general, Hamann also cleared the way for Christianity, which he himself attained to only after a struggle. It was unreasonable, he said, to deny from the standpoint of natural thought, truths whose function it is, not only to overlap all natural human conceptions, but positively to appear as folly to human wisdom. Here he was very near Pascal, who said it was the function of reason to know that innumerable matters lay outside its range, and only a weak reason was blind to its own limitations.[1] Hamann put it more bluntly: If a worshipper of reason was not able to penetrate into the mysterious truth of Christianity, he ought at least to be reasonable enough not to pass judgement on what is out of his reach. It was his Christian conscience that

---

[1] Strowski Ed. Pascal, *Pensées*, 55, 56.

turned Hamann against the *Aufklärung*. Seeing the Christian truths systematically explained away or flatly denied, he became the apologist of Christianity. He took his Christianity from Lutheranism and nourished it on Martin Luther's form of religion, none the less his works remain free of confessional polemics. But a wholly new situation had arisen. In the time of confessional controversy, doctrine opposed doctrine, Church opposed Church, Catholic Christianity opposed Protestant Christianity. With Hamann and after him, the problem shifted. Now, belief opposed unbelief, Christianity opposed non-Christianity. In this new situation, Luther became for Hamann the symbol of faith and of all that was Christian. This distinguished him fundamentally from Herder, with whom he is so readily bracketed. Herder held that his belief in humanity found support in Luther. Hamann was constantly being brought back by Luther to the very heart of Christianity. Herder merely had a feeling for Luther's humanity and a vague religiosity, Hamann, however, for what was intrinsically Christian in him: ' We have not learnt as much from this great man as we might have done and ought to have done—not only in German but in every way.'—' What a shame it is for our times that the spirit of this man who founded our Church lies buried under ashes.' In later years he appealed to Luther on all occasions: ' My disgust with all the undertakings of this age increases. I am now in *Luther* Part VI, and this constitutes my sole occupation at the moment.' Christianity and Lutheranism were, he said, the implicit subject of all his work, over a period of twenty-five years.

(c) CHRISTIAN THOUGHT AND CHRISTIAN HUMANISM

In the age of orthodoxy, Christianity had meant Lutheranism. In the age of the *Aufklärung*, what was meant by Christianity as purified of superstition by Luther, was a more or less natural, human, rational-moralizing religiosity (when it was not turned down lock, stock and barrel, as nonsense). But Hamann meant by Lutheranism, revealed Christianity. Thus it was not confined to confessional Lutheranism, but rather Luther's Church and writings were the way through to what was specifically Christian;

so that for Hamann, at bottom, Lutheranism merged in Christianity. In the second half of the eighteenth century, here was a man with the courage to approach Luther from the Christian standpoint, insisting that Luther could only be rightly understood in a Christian context. This was possible only to Johann Georg Hamann, who had a Christian focus that the others lacked.

How far the Christian in him took precedence of the confessional Lutheran is clear in his criticism of the *Aufklärung*. The Christian principles with which he confronted the claims of natural religion could equally well have come from a devout Catholic. In spite of his harsh words on the ' papacy,' he was not only not anti-Catholic but was conscious of strong Catholic sympathies wherever he found Catholicism backed by Christianity. He proved it in his own person. The last years of his life he spent at Münster in Westphalia at the home of Princess Gallitzin, who was the heart and soul of a circle of ardent Christians, the fount of a devotional revival within Catholicism with repercussions reaching far into the nineteenth century.

Maintaining the primacy of the supernatural and grace, of mystery and the truth of religious faith, over all worldly values, giving the Bible the precedence over all human speculations because it was the word of God, Hamann represented in a world more and more exclusively concentrated upon itself, a Christian standpoint which has at all times been fundamentally the standpoint of Catholicism. For he affirmed the possibility of a Christian attitude of mind in modern times, putting this possibility into effect in his own life and works. What was ' modern ' about it was that it had to be done in surroundings where non-belief was on the increase. Holding good against the gathering main-stream, concentrating meditatively on the facts of divine revelation, this Christian attitude of mind gained poise and discrimination empowering it to understand and withstand the world about it. Standards for judging world and man were, it insisted, to be had from God, so it stood in uncompromising opposition to secular modern thought which took its standards from its notions of man, personality, world, and sought therewith to build up its ideas of God.

The widening gap between belief and unbelief, supernatural and secular, effaced to some extent the differences between the confessions. The secular spirit was inimical to all Christian confessions alike, and in all confessions it was only conscious Christians who understood this. Indifferent Christians of all confessions, used as they were to be carried with the tide, were caught unawares in the ubiquitous trend to secularization. In the Middle Ages and in the times of the wars of religion this did not happen because the world in general was Christian. A non-Christian world had now, however, become a fact, affecting particularly things of the spirit and of the mind. Hence anyone whose attitude of mind was determined by his Christian faith had deliberately to keep clear of the pervading atmosphere if he wanted his faith to remain unsullied and clear—an attitude common, of course, to *all* Christians whose life was grounded on their faith.

The worldly point of view that remakes God in its own image and takes itself for the measure of all things has no doubt constantly recurred from the very beginning of time as a counter-attraction to religion, as is plainly to be seen on almost every page of the Old Testament. The godless power that appeared as the Servant of Baal in the Old Testament and the Whore of Babylon in the New, was to Hamann just as energetically at work in his own time, only he adopted Luther's name for it: papacy. Luther, he remarked, is the ' German Elias and the renewer of Christianity distorted by the Babylonian Baal in idolatrous mass-vestments.' He was not, however, referring to the other confession but to the anti-God principle of enlightened reason. No more can we give a confessional bias to his words, two years before his death, to a friend of Jacobi's, Heinrich Schenk: that his whole authorship ' contained nothing but an Evangelical Lutheranism *in petto* '; or his last fragmentary writing, a passionate confession of faith: ' like the cherubim on either side of the seat of grace,' Christianity and Lutheranism ' spread their wings over the hidden witness of his authorship and its ark of the covenant.' Hamann it was who showed how a Christianity shrunk to a mere matter of formal adherence could still be retrieved if it were lived again and consistently applied. We have here an event of immense significance for modern times, unique because the heartening sense of fellow-membership of the Christian communion that still throve in the days of religious controversy, had died out, leaving each man solitary and alone. The new relation of isolated individual to Church and Christianity was more complicated and differentiated, because each had to learn to make his own approach, but more human, because the rigid dogmatic system relaxed. Thus there was room for a genuine Christian humanism, of which Hamann after his conversion bore traces. He wrote then to his friend Lindner:

A certain leaning to freedom is to some extent more natural to me than to you, and therefore I love Christianity, it suits my sensibility, and claims, and engages, not a pillar of salt but a man. Where God's spirit is found is freedom. And truth makes us free. Righteousness in Christ is no straight-waistcoat but a coat-of-armour to which a warrior grows as accustomed as a Mæcenas to his flowing robes.

When in the name of humanity the *Aufklärung* rejected the Christian creed, Hamann declared that it was the human in him that craved for the supernatural order of salvation. The insight and experience of advancing years speak in the following:

The folly of Christianity is exactly to my taste and heart's desire, acceptable to my sound reason and my human feeling, as is the majesty of the Father and Judge of the world, so that all the botching and bungling of our century are nothing but the immense blot and stigma of its ignorance and insolence.

Hamann, loyal Lutheran that he was, represented a Christianity firmly rooted in the faith and full of life and conviction, and so he found fruitful common ground with a like-minded Catholicism, likewise occupied in fanning embers to fresh life.

Any estimation of Hamann that is to do him justice must start from his Christian faith as the centre-point of his existence.

Goethe, in the twelfth book of *Wahrheit und Dichtung*, shows more concern with the outward effect, recalling the

> worthy influential man . . . who was as great a mystery to us at that time, as to the Fatherland he has always remained. His *Socratic Memoirs* created a sensation and were particularly attractive to those unable to come to terms with the dazzling spirit of the age. One divined the presence of a deep-thinking and scrupulous mind, of a man well aware of the accessible world and literature of his time, but with something mysterious, unaccountable, about him, and who spoke of this in a highly characteristic manner.

Goethe first considered the moment appropriate for more detailed utterances on this author's nature and personality when an edition of his works was under consideration. He inferred he knew the principle, nevertheless, ' to which all that Hamann says can be traced.' It was, he said, ' this: " Whatever a man undertakes to do, whether by means of deed or word or anything else, must arise from his entire united powers; whatever is sporadic is reprehensible." An excellent maxim! but hard to adhere to.' The point of view is entirely worldly, leaving the religious question open and suppressing the Christian one. The general impression given does not really do Hamann justice. The Catholic Princess Gallitzin came much nearer the mark. Her testimony corresponds to the Hamann we find in his works, testifying to the strength of his personality and going to the heart of the matter. It shall therefore close our chapter on the Magus of the North.

The Princess was writing to Friedrich Heinrich Jacobi, the friend of Lessing, Goethe and Hamann, on February 17, 1785:

> What attracted me altogether powerfully to Hamann were our friends in common, Plato, Homer, Socrates, and above all Holy Scripture, in which his whole being is impregnated. With this, very specially, which has in the last years become for me the richest source of life, and almost the only nourishment of my soul, and which after the twentieth reading

remains just as fresh as ever, and each time lights a new light in my soul—to my mind a greater miracle than all the miracles of which it is the first written witness—with this Hamann made his appearance in my company, and in a manner that I am not able to put into words in a letter, wove himself in, so that I became sick as though of some hidden stirring of love for him, that made me want to know him better.

RECAPITULATION AND CONCLUSION

1. THE EIGHTEENTH CENTURY AND LUTHER

IF we compare the seventeenth-century picture of Luther with the multiple forms it took in the eighteenth century, it is obvious that the former had a coherent conception which was later lost sight of. In the seventeenth century the defence of Luther still meant to a large extent the defence of Lutheran Christianity as an absolute, against Calvinism and Catholicism and all other forms of religion. This ceased in the eighteenth century, but then began the fierce battle as to the true Luther within the Lutheran world itself. In the seventeenth century the dogmatic point of view as a rule decided the issue; in the eighteenth it ceased to be generally accepted. The conservative forces in German Lutheranism kept it alive, but conservative orthodoxy itself was driven onto the defensive, gradually or rapidly losing ground. In countless variations and nuances, the spirit of the age found expression in the religious sphere through pietism, in the intellectual sphere through rationalism. The new ideas provided the measure for a new estimation of Luther, whence the views which ever since the late eighteenth century have coloured popular literature and public opinion.

The changes undergone since the seventeenth century were enormous. The directions taken and the deeper underlying motives must here be recalled to mind if the far-reaching nature of the transformation is to be appreciated.

The main element of the metamorphosis was a quite definite shift of opinion to the detriment of orthodoxy. It was no longer held that Luther propounded, as one and only, a faith on which absolute salvation depended. Luther was now honoured as the champion of freedom. Again and again we read it: he brought freedom from outward constraint, freedom of thought and conscience. His scruples, temptations and calls to penance were hardly mentioned, the stress was on his exemplary manhood—its power, feeling and heart; on his admirable ardour, and on his all too evident—and deplorable—fanaticism. One should, as we further read, take him as an example, but not indiscriminately. Not, for instance, his reactionary faith in the letter—which was roundly termed superstition—nor his intolerant insistence on a special ' doctrine,' but his good intention, the impulsive nature of his piety, the natural buoyancy of his way of life. His ' spirit ' was readily contrasted with the ' letter ' of his doctrine. Dogma was discarded, but the dynamic personality made a great effect. Thus the final verdict was on the whole a positive one.

But Luther was in favour for other reasons too. The *Aufklärung* historian, Johann Matthias Schröckh (1733–1808), puts it as follows:

> He preached a doctrine which seemed the right one for upholding the dignity of rulers and maintaining peace in the State. After an experience of two centuries, it should be common knowledge throughout Europe that the Protestant religion is the only one taking into consideration the legitimate powers and proper privileges of princes; as is well known, the Evangelical Churches have allowed them in particular many rights in regard to spiritual matters. With the assurance natural to a man of his merits, Luther held that if he had done or taught nothing else of worth, he was yet deserving of thanks and favour for the way he had enlightened and adorned secular government or royal authority. And we may confidently repeat: if the Reformation had done the world no other service . . . it could still lay claim to the gratitude of all princes and also of all subjects. . . . That royal authority regained possession of all that the tyrants of the Church for so long withheld from it; further that religion was tarnished by no seeds of unrest; and that the government of our princes, freed from commands and threats, from excommunication and other insolent acts of violence of an Italian bishop, could now be of unmitigated benefit to their subjects: all this was without doubt Luther's work.[1]

[1] J. M. Schröckh: *Representations and Descriptions of the Lives of Famous Men*, Vol. II, 1766, pp. 68 sq. (No. 33: Martin Luther).

Briefly, it was Luther's merit to have set aside the authoritarian Church; freed the State from outside interference and the human person from external constraint; and established the right to freedom of thought and conscience. Thus, on account of his services to State and individual, an unique benefactor of the human race was in Luther deserving of honour.[1]

As a matter of fact, any judgement pronounced on Luther rebounds upon the Reformation and Protestantism. The *Aufklärung* had a positive attitude to the Reformation corresponding to its positive attitude to Luther—and on both accounts found itself at cross purposes with orthodoxy.

Orthodoxy had defined the Reformation in a strictly spiritual sense: as a miraculous intervention of God in history for the salvation of Christendom. The *Aufklärung* defined it as a revolution of humanity and saw it as the beginning of a mighty movement for setting the human spirit free; a revolution of religious individualism against ecclesiastical constraint; a revolution of science in search of freedom, as against scholasticism bound in dogma. Thus the Reformation came to be the herald of the enlightenment and the beginning of that evolution of progress which the enlightened mind of the eighteenth century felt itself called to carry to perfection.

The course of the Reformation was interpreted, not theologically, but historically, the elucidation of it was based on pre-suppositions of a purely natural and historical order. True, the idea of a wise providence working through natural means was not turned down out of hand.[2] But the prevailing idea was that the Reformation was the result of man's purposeful planning. Its origin was, it was supposed, the right of mankind to freedom.

---

[1] At the end of the eighteenth century, Luther's German-ness was to be discovered. He will thus be allotted a special place of honour in the rising national movement. We observe how in Herder Luther's concern for the nation takes precedence over his concern for the Gospel: a point of view that set a precedent for the nineteenth century.

[2] Cf. Schiller, *On the Migration of Peoples, Crusades and Middle Ages*. His small historical essays of the Jena period are in particular typical products of enlightened historical thought.

And its achievements were described as, in the political sphere, the regional church system and prince-episcopacies, and in the theological sphere, the principle of variability of doctrine and the right to private religion—all acclaimed as landmarks on the road of progress. It was customary to mention that the Reformation had undertaken the moral improvement of mankind, but with the corollary that in this respect it had come short of the mark, and the task had to be taken over by posterity. Last but not least, the Reformation was seen as the historic starting-point of tolerance and humanity, the first stirring of the world-wide freedom-movement in man and State, the creative re-birth of culture and true Christianity. All in all, the launching of a process of evolution towards a goal of perfection at once reasonable, natural and human. One was immensely conscious that the *Aufklärung* continued the Reformation, as indeed appeared likely for the beginnings of the *Aufklärung* were commonly projected back on to the Reformation.

In general there was no hesitation in calling Luther ' the founder of our improved religion,' but a more or less sharp distinction was made, especially in the second half of the century, between Luther and the existing Lutheran Church in so far as it laid claim to dogmatic orthodoxy. Semler and Lessing make this very plain.

On one point, it is true, Luther was often called to witness: to support the view that the conduct of the Church ought to be entrusted to the State. But this gave rise to very un-Lutheran ideas, as is highly apparent if we recall the Church idea of Lutheran-orthodox imprint, for instance in Johann Gerhard and Valentin Ernst Löscher. They defined the Church as the communion of those acknowledging the true faith and conform-ing to established custom and the order of sacraments, but laid it down that the true faith was set out in the *Confessio Augustana*: thus confining the Church in principle to the communion of the Augsburg Confession. It was precisely this homogeneity between Church and *Confessio Augustana* that the *Aufklärung* queried as a matter of principle. The most useful thinking was done perhaps by Semler, who made the following distinction:

a Church community may well be founded outwardly on a given 'doctrine'—the Augsburg or any other confession—but it may never oblige its members as individuals to observe the official doctrine to the letter. For on 'doctrine' (how un-Lutheran!) salvation can never depend. Thus to insist on obligation in relation to doctrine is impermissible interference with the conscience and private religion of the individual.

Here is a highlight on the phenomenon of personal piety in process of detaching itself from established Church belief. What is significant is less the separation itself than the devaluation entailed: of the two, private religion was to be preferred. There was no need for Church teaching to be binding on the individual, for the Church was after all only there to safeguard outward order in religious matters: there was no longer any notion of a guardian and propagator of eternal truth.

On the other hand, from Seckendorf through Spener to Semler, we have the constant factor of an all-embracing invisible Church. The idea was, however, subject to progressive sublimation and tended to disappear into thin air. In Semler the visible and invisible Churches seem to exist side by side with no apparent contact. The invisible Church detaches itself from the visible one.

But the visible Church loses its *raison d'être* when it has merely an outward, almost technical function, that of maintaining order. Such was the opinion of Frederick the Great, Möser and Schröckh, and it appeared quite logical to reject as sheer arrogance all claims of the Church to religious authority. And no one can logically avoid seeing as further consequence, the assumed competence of the State to play a part in Church government and to count on practical assistance from such an appropriate institution for ruling and instructing its subjects.

Autonomy of State and autonomy of individual were taken for granted. State and individual were thus disinclined to allow the Church any right to a sphere of influence that might affect them. The idea of the invisible Church faded into the blue, and the visible Church was conceived as so ponderous that the notion of submitting to it denoted lack of personal independence or a die-hard attitude, if not downright hypocrisy due to ambition or cunning. In the great age of German poetry and philosophy it was self-evident that one could get along perfectly well without the Church.

2. THE SECULARIZATION OF RELIGION

It goes without saying that the metamorphoses in the Evangelical estimation of Luther, Reformation and Church had a common root, in the great process of secularization that was going on throughout the western world. Variations in stress were all symptoms pointing to the fact that the Christian religion as such was in the throes of crisis. For Christianity infers, on the part of man, belief, and in the eighteenth century it was no longer possible to believe. At any rate very many people were no longer capable of it. The leading minds of the century were in the main so utterly incapable of belief that it was impossible for them to accept the traditional form of ecclesiastical orthodox Christianity.

From this state of affairs two possibilities emerged. Either, as a clear consequence of inaptitude to believe, you relinquished Christianity altogether: this was the point of view of Frederick the Great and in the end of Lessing too. Or as a compromise you relinquished the formulated content of faith and turned your Christianity into a non-dogmatic religion. That meant freeing religion, Church and theology from the creeds of revealed Christianity but keeping the name ' Christian.' The result was to reduce Christianity to its ethic—culminating in the acceptance of Christian ethics only in so far as identifiable with natural ethics. This second way, the way of compromise, so much more equivocal than the first, is the way most people chose.

Hence the new interpretation of Christianity characteristic of modern times. The transformation did not take place in a rapid succession of mutations, but rather in the patient, often wearisome, poring over minute points of detail of whole generations of theologians. Leaf after leaf, secularism shed all traces of formulated faith.

The process is in one sense not easy to follow because the

terms in common use did not change when the changes in value called the new tune, the tendency was to go on quite naïvely using the traditional vocabulary, and when words like truth, faith, religion appear, one may be fairly sure they express something quite different from the traditional Christian meaning.

Awed by the spirit of the age, the Evangelical theologians took pains to explain the supernatural revealed truths of faith as 'natural' and 'reasonable' truths, and to establish that Christianity was nothing but a natural religion, a purely historical event. A Christianity under the yoke of a superimposed historical law was a transitional stage in the course of man's evolution towards perfection.

In this sense it was the Lutheran form of Christianity that represented progress. It was said to have the advantage of hindering no one from advancing in personal knowledge of truth as each saw fit. Indeed it was to Luther himself that one was indebted for the right to form one's own idea of Christianity and religion. The original communal religion was thus splintered into a thousand fragments of private piety, each with the character and form of individual taste. Christianity, no longer understood as acknowledgement of the inherent facts of a common faith, was taken to depend on the genuineness of a person's religious intention.

For this the *Aufklärung* is directly responsible. But to turn Christianity into a purely private matter is to foster secularization. 'Religion,' confined to man's inner experience, is a relative thing conditioned by a subjective sense of veracity and out of contact with absolute truth. The truth of the New Testament tradition, said Lessing, by which he meant the historical events recorded in the Gospels, is of far less interest than the 'inner' truth of religion. But 'inner truth' is wholly dependent on the feeling, attitude and opinion of the individual.

That is the heart of the crisis in the religion of the western world. Man formerly allowed himself to learn from revelation and Church what manner of creature he was; now he had to seek the measure of godly things in himself. Church, doctrine and Scripture were to be submitted to the judgement of his reason, a judgement standardized by his views on his own human existence, personality and social obligations. In direct opposition to tradition, religion now no longer overhung and embraced the world, but was included in the world as one among other phenomena. No longer specifically itself, it was soon merely another name for virtue, feeling, probity.

Thus, in short, religion was bereft of its Christian character, though the term ' Christian ' was left.

3. EFFECTS AND CONSEQUENCES

(a) SYNTHESIS OF PROTESTANTISM AND SECULARISM

Freedom of conscience, in terms of freedom of thought and doctrine, was the lever used to lift the Christian idea off its hinges. The Evangelical writers all held unmistakably that the turning of religion into a private concern was a specifically Protestant development, giving wide application to the principle of freedom of conscience derived from Luther. Thus emancipation of thought and shift of focus were both fruits of Luther's protest. The consequences were immense. In the nineteenth century, Protestantism and the spirit of progress went hand in hand, often taken as identical.[1] Freedom from obligation was of the very nature of Protestantism—or so it was assumed. There was too a vestige of the old familiar equation of Lutheran Protestantism as identical with true Christianity, in the current idea that this volatilized form of religion was essentially Protestant and therefore truly Christian. Protestantism thus acquired a certain turn of character, inwardly secular, outwardly Christian, which has since caused it some misgivings, as is very evident in the discussions of the Evangelical Churches among one another in the twentieth century.

(b) THE DOUBLE POLARITY OF PROTESTANTISM

The Lutheran Reformation, which began as a profoundly spiritual Christian movement, resulted in the eighteenth century in a perversion of the words of the Bible (Luther's life-work having

[1] Whereas Catholicism was considered hopelessly behind the times.

been the restoration of the Bible) and a topsyturvy turning of Christianity: these are plain facts which cannot be denied.

According to Lessing, it was outstandingly good Lutheran to abandon the exact principles of faith which Luther had so scrupulously laid down. The *Aufklärung* writers proclaimed their respect for Luther, and setting out in a contrary direction, insisted that they were following in his footsteps. As the Catholic theologian Johann Adam Möhler said, early in the nineteenth century: the Protestant theologians of his time acknowledged their debt to Luther ' only in that he had won them freedom to believe exactly the opposite of what he and the communion he founded believed.'[1]

The historian cannot but observe how early the two principles of Protestantism came apart and developed separately. In orthodoxy the doctrinal principle maintained itself powerfully as an historical reality. Whereas the principle of freedom of conscience became lop-sided in the age of the *Aufklärung*, and the nineteenth and twentieth centuries played havoc with what was left of it.

Protestantism's two underlying principles may in extreme cases be mutually exclusive. There were not only extremes, however, but a number of transitional and conciliatory forms too. But in all situations one or other of the two was dominant and determined the issue. Where one was active, the other was latent. Luther's free conscience and the idea of personal enlightenment—a consequence of his recriminations against the ruling Church of his day—was far more actual to the hosts of enthusiasts, baptists and sectarians of the Reformation century than fear of an orthodoxy enjoying the support of State and inquisition. It was the sectarians who safeguarded and handed on the spiritual estate which later became the happy hunting-ground of pietists and *aufklärer*. On the other hand, when *Aufklärung* biblical criticism and religious liberalism held the field, the Lutheran parishes with orthodox pastors, though reduced in number, did not go out of existence, but were the trustees of most valuable

[1] J. A. Möhler, *Symbolik*, Preface to 1st edition (1832); p. xi of the 8th and 9th editions (1913).

Lutheran material, maintaining unimpaired their allegiance to ' the doctrine.'

But whichever principle was dominant at the time, the two together were uncomfortable bed-fellows. Inherently so. Their incompatibility, running as it does right through the history of Protestantism, may be traced back to the paradoxes evident in Luther himself. In spite of all deviations, something of Luther still haunted the minds of *Aufklärung* theologians.[1] Pietism and rationalism are possibly to be understood as a sublimation of Luther's protest. Or, for instance, a re-awakening of it in a narrower field: as the protest of the Evangelical individual against any form of guardianship by the Evangelical Church. In fact, as the turning of Luther's protest against the very Church that arose out of it.

To sum up: viewed historically, Protestantism is inherently of two kinds. First there was the rejection of Church authority in favour of personal experience, based historically on Luther's rejection of the old Church in the name of his conscience, and since the eighteenth century declared by the Protestants to be the main principle of Lutheran Protestantism. Then there was the whole-hearted acceptance of the content of biblical doctrine, the ' pure doctrine ' proclaimed by Luther. This was the Protestantism of the Lutheran Christians particularly in the sixteenth and seventeenth centuries, admitting complete identification of Luther's teaching with the word of God, holding for true that same creed that Luther held for true.

Now the contrast between these two kinds of Protestantism is in the long run so great that the difference between a doctrinal Protestantism and doctrinal Catholicism may pale in comparison, and the partial but none the less real agreement, in the light of all that separates the Protestantism of private experience from dogmatic Protestantism, can only be termed fundamental.[2]

---

[1] Heinz Fluegel (*Hochland*, 39th Year, Vol. 4, p. 373, Note 6) points out that traces of Lutheran influence have been discovered even in Nietzsche.

[2] For clarity on this point we are indebted to a work of Helmut Groos, *German Idealism and Christianity* (Munich, 1927): a confrontation of Luther and Thomas Aquinas on the one hand, and the ideas underlying German literature of the classical period, on the other.

(c) THE QUESTION OF THE SECULAR PROTESTANT CONSCIENCE

This is a real Christian problem. When, as is not impossible, conscience drives a man to give up Luther's doctrine as set down in the Augsburg Confession, on account of profound personal experience of another kind, when it is really done for conscience' sake, is he not in fact undergoing the same experience as Luther underwent when he cut loose from the Catholic Church and doctrine? The rights that Luther had belong to us all, said Lessing, Semler, Herder; they would welcome such deviation from the doctrinal way not only as good and right, but also as Lutheran. But in practice deviation from Lutheran doctrine for Lutheran motives leads away from Luther. The alternative may be Calvinism, or Catholicism, or it may be a material philosophy or nihilism. So a Lutheran acting on Lutheran motives might turn nihilist or atheist—for to act on conviction is to copy Luther. The nineteenth century has more than sufficient evidence of the fact that Evangelical theologians did not believe in the divinity of Christ: it was against their conviction to do so. There was no question here of identity of agreement with Luther's teaching, but they none the less described themselves as Protestants; and were able to do so simply because they held as ' Protestant ' Luther's own example in the matter of freedom of personal choice.

Thus there is no straightforward answer as to the nature of Lutheran Christianity.

If the answer is that it is grounded in Holy Scripture, the question immediately arises, who has the right to interpret Holy Scripture authoritatively? Old Lutherans inclined to say, Luther alone. But to say so is to admit that Luther's doctrine based on Scripture, being authoritative, has authority over the individual conscience, and does not leave room for personal readings into Scripture that differ from Luther's. Pietism and rationalism pointed derisively and relentlessly to the consequence: Lutheran doctrine, rigidly adhered to, does violence to the conscience of the individual, as regards his freedom to take God's word quite personally and in whatever form best suits him.

But if the answer is that Lutheran Christianity is the right
to freedom of choice subject to conscience, then in practice the
application of that right may lead a man very far away from the
faith Luther considered necessary for salvation. There are eight-
eenth- and nineteenth-century examples of what happens when
Bible-interpretation becomes a matter of private judgement with
no given standards to guide it: it may lead right outside the
Christian sphere, where Luther and Christianity have no more
to say.

Thus the question-mark at the heart of Protestantism coincides
with the presence of these two principles which met in Luther
but refuse to be reconciled as historical facts, and if given free
play act each to the detriment of the other, so that it is possible
to say, Protestantism contains the seed of its own destruction.

(d) THE SECULAR CONSCIENCE : A NEW SITUATION

Protestantism part Christian, part non-Christian

History shows that the more firmly Protestantism takes
its stand on its dogmatic belief, the more surely it safeguards its
innate Christian character. Whereas with the discarding of dogma
arises the danger of de-Christianization.

The more, let it be said, it concentrates on the content of its
faith, the greater grows the possibility of a true confrontation
between it and Catholicism which, as is well known, disallows
the Protestant claim to possess in its doctrine the whole only-
saving truth. Should such a confrontation take place, the
Protestant line would be to take Scripture as its base to prove
the reliability of its own articles of faith and to test those of
Catholic dogma. The Catholic approach would naturally be
from the idea of the Church, by which all stands or falls. If the
Church could be proved wrong in its claims—a thing the Catholic
believer could never accept as possible—then the right to lapse
from the Church under given conditions could not be turned
down out of hand; but it would not necessarily mean that
Luther always, in every case, included the whole of biblical
truth in his doctrine. In fact a more likely consequence would

be, for all to be right, or all to be wrong—for no one could say with certainty where truth lay. On the other hand, if the Church cannot err in matters of faith, then the whole controversy comes to an end without any special argument having to take place on the justification doctrine. The question would solve itself, whether any one individual, by appealing to his conscience and his own understanding of Scripture, could accuse the Church of crude error, and on that account be justified in summoning Christianity to turn away from the Church and its teaching.

Be this as it may, let us admit that the eighteenth century did bring about certain preliminary conditions of great value for the future chances of a coming-together. Intolerant and exclusive confessionalism was put down once for all when pietism proclaimed the all-embracing idea of *pietas* as more important than the closed doors of the confessions, and again when rationalism took the wind out of its sails by declaring dogma to be a trifling matter in comparison with reason and virtue—those highly esteemed values accessible to every man regardless of confession.

Since that day, *pietas*, *ethos* and *ratio* have cleared the ground for an understanding between people holding different *Weltanschauungen*. And within the framework of more general meetings, where in the first instance dogmatic differences are not touched upon, meetings of individuals belonging to different confessions are not only possible but have in fact already borne fruit.[1] Early *rapprochements* were not necessarily of great import from the religious point of view, first because they were not undertaken out of religious motives, and next, because they were only possible on account of the small importance attached by all concerned to the separating factor as such. But whatever the motives were at the time, the fact of the coming together opened out wide fields of possibility for future discussions in common. Actually, discussion between confessions will more likely bear fruit when not so much immediate agreement is sought, as

[1] Cf. already in the early nineteenth century H. Steffens' report on his religious talks with Michael Sailer, later Bishop of Regensburg, in: Steffens, *Was ich erlebte* (What I experienced), Leipzig, 1938, Coll. Dietrich, pp. 406 sqq.)

elucidation of that long misunderstood and very actual theme, dogmatic principles.

It was pioneer work in a world which had moved far away from everything Christian. The question, Christian or non-Christian, had now become so acute that the older alternative, Catholic or Protestant, had lost its urgency in comparison. Changes in the general situation put the confessions in an entirely new relation to one another.

With the appearance on the scene of Hamann and Herder, the stage was set. These two men between them, representing contrasting views, differing in power and status, are more or less patently responsible for the whole religious tension of the nineteenth and twentieth centuries in Germany.

On the one hand, Herder, the representative of ' natural ' humanity, whose quickening influence on idealism and romanticism and on the national and liberal movements of the following century can hardly be exaggerated. His views on nation and history, ' natural ' human nature, and ' natural ' religion determined by personality, local custom, language and humanity, met with widespread approval and were multiplied in a thousand echoes. The thinkers and poets of the Goethe period accepted the complete re-estimation of basic human values as a matter of course. In fact if intellectual life had not been by then completely secularized, the philosophy and poetry of the age of German idealism would never have come into existence. The question whether religion is transcendental or immanent was vehemently discussed during the *Aufklärung*—but for Herder and the classical period that followed, it was no longer valid.[1] German classical literature was so imbued with the immanence of religion and the ideal of dogma-free Christianity that any other possibility was unthinkable. In the classical literature and in idealism there are no traces of resistance to religious liberalism and the materialistic *Weltanschauung* which were to dominate the intellectual evolution of the nineteenth and twentieth centuries. Rather they

[1] H. A. Korff, *Geist der Goethezeit* (The spirit of the Age of Goethe), Vol. I, p. 276: " With Lessing and Goethe the history of the German mind enters its pagan period. This is an incontestable fact."

must be seen as fellow-accomplices with German classicism and idealism in their negation of Christianity in its right to engage a man.

Hamann appears in the vanguard of the movement that set in against this negation. Here was no insistence on a naural autonomy of man, as in Herder. But rather a vision of how an overpowering longing for supernatural reality can sweep across the boundaries of ' nature.' For Hamann, human existence is wholly and utterly bent towards the God of revelation of the Old and New Testaments, in whom the most real reality is to be found, and from whom the *Nomos* for a man's own existence can in faith be received. Hamann's ' humanity ' differs fundamentally from the contemporary classical-natural notions, it is based on a theocentric order of life, whereas *Aufklärung*, classicism and idealism founded their anthropocentric view of the world on a presumption of human autonomy. Hamann sharply emphasized the incompatibility of such views with a genuine Christian outlook.

The classical thinkers and poets were Protestants born and bred. Herder was even a theologian. Hamann was a Protestant too. From now on there is a dividing wall. It is more than symptomatic that Hamann had his talks on the faith, not with Herder and Goethe, but with Princess Gallitzin, a Catholic.

In the nineteenth century, what was characteristic in men like Renan, Nietzsche, Feuerbach, was not the religious denomination to which they once belonged, but the anti-Christian nature of their ideas.

In Grillparzer and Stifter too, both of Catholic origin, and in the Protestants Burckhardt and Fontane, what is significant is not the confession but the direction in which their thoughts on religion, Christianity and Church tended to run.

And even in downright Christian figures of the nineteenth century, such as Eichendorff and der Droste, the Protestant Jeremias Gotthelf and the Catholic Anton Bruckner, what marked them out as withstanding the trend of their century was not specific membership of a Church but their Christian way of life. Indeed these men (and many others unnamed)—

o*

loyal adherents of their respective confessions—all experienced in their life that growth of prudence and power they knew to be necessary for the ordering of it.

It is a true and remarkable phenomenon that in the nineteenth century members of various confessions should have preached and practised a Christian way of life wholly uninfluenced by the ' liberal ' spirit of the time; a way of life traceable to precisely those norms sponsored alike by active professing Protestant denominations and the entire Catholic Church as such.

Since the nineteenth century, more important than actual membership of a denomination appears to be the attitude of the individual to the content of religion and confessional faith. Christianity, historically speaking, has once again entered on a new phase, a new relation to the world. It can no longer be assumed that true professing Christians are found only within the fold of the one Church—as in the Middle Ages; or attached to a given denomination—as in the reformed confessional period; they are wherever man as individual has come face to face with Christian reality in the faith, and has taken it on as the guiding principle in his life. And thus, whatever in the confessions is husk and not kernel is slowly, as it seems, peeling off. Short of error, that will mean for Luther's Church a stronger reliance on its professing members than in the last century-and-a-half, and an acceptance of more positive institutional forms (for the main-tenance of the Church as such, and of rite and faith), resulting in a visible transformation all to its credit. The signs are not lacking.

INDEX

217